MW00473937

Finding Language and Imagery

Elements of Preaching

O. Wesley Allen Jr., series editor

Thinking Theologically
The Preacher as Theologian
Ronald J. Allen

Knowing the Context
Frames, Tools, and Signs for Preaching
James R. Nieman

Interpreting the Bible
Approaching the Text in Preparation for Preaching
Mary F. Foskett

Shaping the Claim
Moving from Text to Sermon
Marvin A. McMickle

Determining the Form
Structures for Preaching
O. Wesley Allen Jr.

Finding Language and Imagery
Words for Holy Speech
Jennifer L. Lord

Delivering the Sermon
Voice, Body, and Animation in Proclamation
Teresa L. Fry Brown

Serving the Word
Preaching in Worship
Melinda A. Quivik

Finding Language and Imagery

and Imagery

Words for Holy Speech

Jennifer L. Lord

Fortress Press

Minneapolis

FINDING LANGUAGE AND IMAGERY
Words for Holy Speech

Copyright © 2010 Fortress Press, an imprint of Augsburg Fortress. All rights reserved.
Except for brief quotations in critical articles or reviews, no part of this book may
be reproduced in any manner without prior written permission from the publisher.
Visit http://www.augsburgfortress.org/copyrights/contact.asp or write to Permissions,
Augsburg Fortress, Box 1209, Minneapolis, MN 55440.

Scripture passages are from the New Revised Standard Version of the Bible, copyright
© 1989 National Council of the Churches of Christ in the USA. Used by permission.
All rights reserved.

Cover image: © iStockphoto.com/Igor Skrynnikov
Cover and book design: John Goodman

Library of Congress Cataloging-in-Publication Data
Lord, Jennifer L., 1965–
  Finding language and imagery : words for holy speech / Jennifer L. Lord.
    p. cm. — (elements of preaching)
  Includes bibliographical references.
  ISBN 978-0-8006-6353-7 (alk. paper)
  1. Preaching. 2. Oral communication—Religious aspects—Christianity. I. Title.
  BV4211.3.L665 2009
  251'.01—dc22
                            2009038342

The paper used in this publication meets the minimum requirements of American National
Standard for Information Sciences—Permanence of Paper for Printed Library Materials,
ANSI Z329.48-1984.

Manufactured in the U.S.A.

14   13   12   11   10   1   2   3   4   5   6   7   8   9   10

Contents

Editor's Foreword

Preparing beginning preachers to stand before the body of Christ and proclaim the word of God faithfully, authentically, and effectively Sunday after Sunday is and always has been a daunting responsibility. As North American pastors face pews filled with citizens of a postmodern, post-Christendom culture, this teaching task becomes even more complex. The theological, exegetical, and homiletical skills that preachers need for the future are as much in flux today as they have ever been in Western Christianity. Thus providing seminary students with a solid but flexible homiletical foundation at the start of their careers is a necessity.

Traditionally, professors of preaching choose a primary introductory textbook that presents a theology of proclamation and a process of sermon development and delivery from a single point of view. To maintain such a singular point of view is the sign of good writing, but it does at times cause problems for learning in pluralistic settings. One approach to preaching does not fit all. Yet a course simply surveying all of the homiletical possibilities available will not provide a foundation on which to build either.

Furthermore, while there are numerous introductory preaching textbooks from which to choose, most are written from the perspective of Euro-American males. Classes supplement this view with smaller homiletical texts written by women and persons of color. But a pedagogical hierarchy is nevertheless set up: the white male voice provides the main course and women and persons of color provide the side dishes.

Elements of Preaching is a series designed to help professors and students of preaching—including established preachers who want to develop their skills in specific areas—construct a sound homiletical foundation in a conversational manner. This conversation is meant to occur at two levels. First, the series as a whole deals with basic components found in most introductory preaching classes: theology of proclamation, homiletical contexts, biblical interpretation, sermonic claim, language and imagery, rhetorical form, delivery, and worship. But each element is presented by a different scholar, all of whom represent diversity in terms of gender, theological traditions (Baptist, Disciple of Christ, Lutheran, Presbyterian, and United Methodist), and ethnicity (African American, Asian American, and Euro-American). Instead of bringing in different voices at the margin of the preaching class, Elements of Preaching creates a conversation around the central topics of an introductory course without foregoing essential instruction concerning sermon construction and embodiment. Indeed, this level of conversation is extended beyond the printed volumes through the Web site www.ElementsofPreaching.com.

Second, the individual volumes are written in an open-ended manner. The individual author's particular views are offered but in a way that invites, indeed demands, the readers to move beyond them in developing their own approaches to the preaching task. The volumes offer theoretical and practical insights, but at the last page it is clear that more must be said. Professors and students have a solid place to begin, but there is flexibility within the class (and after the class in ministry) to move beyond these volumes by building on the insights and advice they offer.

In the week-in and week-out work of preparing and delivering sermons, we preachers can become dull to the full potential that figurative language and stories have to offer congregations a new experience of the gospel. In this volume, Jennifer L. Lord reminds us of this and helps readers appreciate and manage the task of attending closely to sermonic language and imagery. She opens with a theological examination of the gift and dangers inherent in speech and then turns to an overview of communication theories that will help readers locate themselves to preaching in a complex landscape in ways that will help them sharpen their understanding of the purpose of preaching. Next Lord offers readers sound practical guidance for creating and discovering, shaping and speaking, language and images that will enliven the proclamation of the gospel. Finally, she allows us to learn by example by presenting a sermon accompanied by a running commentary that highlights the way she has used imagery and shaped language toward a specific homiletical goal.

O. Wesley Allen Jr.

Introduction and Acknowledgments

Week after week preachers use words. We read them, we write and speak them. We look for the exact words for the moment. They are our means for doing: celebration, lament, explanation, remembrance, justification, anticipation, beseeching, condemnation, comfort. This is all to say that words are our medium for the proclamation of the good news of the Triune God whom we know through Christ Jesus. For most of us this word work is still done through the oral medium of speech. But even preachers who make use of computerized visuals, display screens, and musical interludes still work with words.

We do all of this work in a time of word inflation and overuse. Words do not carry the same stock they once did. But they are our coinage. So chapter 1 looks at the care we must show in choosing and handling words. Chapter 2 maps certain theories of language as a way of exploring the tension between the function of language: Does it reflect or create reality? Chapter 3 presents steps for weekly sermon preparation that help preachers pay attention to word choices. Chapter 4 is a case study of a sermon with commentary about word choices. Chapter 5 is a glossary of additional ways words are used in sermons.

This book is part of a series, and so I depend on readers to put these words in conversation with the other volumes of Elements of Preaching. Moreover, this book is for continuing conversation: the glossary is not exhaustive but should stimulate critical thought about how we use words; the map of language theories is only a nod in the direction of linguistic complexities, but it should raise good questions about our intentions; the other chapters should generate reflection about how careful we are with the content of our speech and in our preparations for preaching speech.

It is an honor to have been asked to work on this project, and I am indebted to David Lott and O. Wesley Allen for that invitation. Wes is an insightful, supportive, and unflappable editor and colleague. And it is a great thing to work again with Fortress Press editor David Lott.

I began this book during my academic sabbatical in 2007–2008; I am grateful to President Theodore J. Wardlaw, Dean Michael Jinkins, and the Trustees of Austin Presbyterian Theological Seminary for sabbatical time.

I also extend my thanks to another seminary community; I was one block away from San Francisco Theological Seminary during those sabbatical months and the faculty and staff folded me in as a visiting professor. I am grateful to the people of St. Nicholas Orthodox Church in America, San Anselmo, who gave my husband and me housing and cheered me on. And in particular to their archpriest, the Very Reverend Stephan Mehol- ick, who was a constant homiletics and liturgics conversation partner. There are those who have shaped the way I think about words; some of them are William and Catherine Lord, Louise Lord Nelson, George P. Rice, the people of First Presbyterian Church of Waterville, New York, Gordon Lathrop, Gail Ramshaw, and my writing partner Melinda Quivik. I give thanks for my husband who is a collaborator in adventure. It is not a small thing to live in mutual forbearance throughout a writing project. Casey Alan Clapp blesses me each day. Finally, I had the gift of living close to my two homiletics mentors: Jana Childers and Linda Clader. They live by what they say. They know there is no such thing as a synonym. And they are committed to the yoke of saying the right words. This book is dedicated to them.

Chapter 1

Choosing Preaching Words

How do we choose preaching words? It is a pertinent question for our time. We live with a glut of words. Books of words are available in hard copy, on CDs, on e-books, and online. Our public buildings and our personalized earphones pipe musical words into our ears. Words via radio commentary are always available. Televised words, in flat-screen format, fit on drugstore checkout countertops, in hair salons, and auto-oil-change waiting rooms. And the Internet keeps us connected to worldwide words: the e-mail, blogs, podcasts, tweets, and social network postings are the particles floating around us at all times. We are now sensitized to this air quality. What are preaching words in the midst of all these words? How do preachers choose words? What will guide our choices?

A few years back a certain churchman, Robert Hovda, was already keen on this issue. Hovda observed how difficult it is for ministers leading worship to edit what comes out of their mouths. He diagnosed the problem: too many ministers sound like the loquacious extremes of talk-show hosts. Hovda declared that ministers should practice "the custody of the tongue" in our culture of incessant commentary.[1]

I think of Hovda's phrase and want to use it this way: the custody of words. For preachers, word choice is an action of custody, or, better, custodianship. I do not mean custodianship in the sense of property rights but in the sense of caretaking. We are custodians of words when we wonder about the best way to say things for a particular gathering of people. What words will make sense to this group of persons? What speech is too harsh? What is not strong enough? We are custodians of speech when we scrutinize daily speech and decide what speech we will borrow. We are custodians of speech when we sift through all the words available to us to find gospel words. Preachers are custodians of holy speech.

This is not easy work. Preaching still carries negative connotations for so many people. It means moral repudiation, an argument, a lecture, a shaming. It is still used pejoratively: "Don't preach at me!" Tell someone you study preaching and you will get a raised-eyebrow response. It sounds antiquated, tedious, or at best imperious.

What are we doing?

Let's start with a look at language. We'll begin with an expansive view of language: preachers are like *all* other human beings—we communicate. Then we will adjust the aperture and examine how preachers are like *some* other humans—we are careful about the words we use. Then we tighten the focus and look at preachers as *a unique group* amidst humans—we choose certain words to proclaim good news. This chapter gives an overview of the ways that preachers work with words.

Choosing Communication

Human beings choose to communicate, and we have worked at this for a long time. Museums around the world protect centuries of evidence of human communication. You can visit the replica cave of Lascaux, France, or an official Web site about it to see how these Paleolithic humans from 40,000 B.C.E. interpreted their surroundings through depictions of humans, animals, and constellations of the night skies. These cave images are evidence that before written language was invented, humans used pictures to communicate. The tombs of the Egyptian kings are similarly like an underground still shot but this time of royal court activities, the life of the gods, and daily life in the land of the Nile. The Egyptians also gave us a regulated pictorial form of a written language that we call hieroglyphics. These messages from 3000 B.C.E. were undecipherable until the late eighteenth century, when the discovery of a block of stone known as the Rosetta Stone revealed the key. The stone was inscribed with three languages, one of which was Greek. Thus, an eighteenth-century scholar was able to make connections between that script and the hieroglyphic inscription. Many scholars believe the cuneiform language of the Sumerians in Mesopotamia is even older than the Egyptian's hieroglyphic script. Researchers still work to date early Chinese and South American scripts. We humans have been at the work of communication for a long time.

Some more recent accounts of language acquisition bring the profundity of communication closer to home. For instance, in William Gibson's play *The Miracle Worker*, the audience meets Helen Keller, who has been without sight or hearing from the age of a year and a half. We meet her just at the time she is brought to a teacher who will break through her isolation. This teacher, Annie Sullivan, uses her own fingers to form certain repeated gestures in the palm of Helen's hand. Again and again Annie will place Helen's hand on an object and then make specific patterns in Helen's hand. One day Annie and Helen are at the water pump to refill a water pitcher, with Annie holding Helen's hand under the spigot as she works the pump. Annie again and again spells the word in Helen's palm: w-a-t-e-r. And then it occurs: the moment of comprehension when Helen connects the gestures patterning her palm with the substance coming from the pump. Now she links the word spelled out in her hand to the object.

Things have identifiers: What we sit in is a chair. What we sleep on is a bed. What we put on our feet are shoes. Communication has happened. At this level of communication, words are our currency for exchanging information. A chair is a chair, a bed a bed, and shoes are shoes. So now we take these identifiers and begin to say things about them. We exchange the currency of words and we express ideas, state opinions, and make our needs and desires known: The chair is uncomfortable. The bed is identical to my sister's. I would like to buy those shoes.

In our time we know that this language-currency work starts right away with babies. The dominant progression of language acquisition occurs at least from infancy, to some extent before that, as the developing fetus begins to recognize the voices most often heard or the music played. Then from birth the baby is immersed in the bath of sights, sounds, gestures, tastes, smells, and touch. All of these associations combine in the child's brain to form the language by which the child will negotiate the world. The child learns the particular alphabet and the number system of her culture, and begins to read and calculate.

Words are a primary means of human interpersonal connection, and we work at making ourselves clear. Persons with certain sensory, physical, or cognitive disabilities—those who are differently abled—make use of augmentative communication methods to achieve careful and exact use of words. Some persons use a sign language that is as full and dynamic as spoken language. Some persons sip and push air through a straw to command their electronic keyboard to serve in place of their vocal chords. Some use picture symbol systems—a picture of a desk means it is time to sit and work, a lunchbox means it is time to eat. Some nod or blink or move their eyes left and right, no and yes, to answer questions asked of them, even to spell out words.

Humans choose to communicate. There are many ways that we work to learn language and to learn new languages. Some of us use augmentative communication devices to help us communicate according to the common spoken language. Some of us learn another country's language in order to facilitate our travel or work. Some of us learn languages in order to read ancient texts. Some of us learn a different language in order to sing particular music. We learn language specific to our jobs enabling us to work in a particular industry. Some persons work to communicate with animals. Others spend time sending communications beyond our planet. Even vows of silence are in service to communication with God or self. We work hard to live a languaged life: to express ourselves and absorb what others are saying to us.

Choosing the Right Words

But language, like all other aspects of life, can overwhelm us. Godfrey Reggio's 1983 film *Koyaanisquatsi* has enjoyed long-term popularity in part because it captures this frenzy of life. Though the film begins with time-lapse sequences of nature (clouds, flowers), it eventually depicts human life and then accelerates to show the untenable human pace that is now so far from the rhythms of nature. *Koyaanisquatsi*, subtitled *Life Out of Balance*, explores imbalance.

Preachers are like all other humans because we participate in the rhythms of communication. But we are also part of a select group of people who know about the excess of words. These days our version of *Koyaanisquatsi* is that tens of thousands of words pass over our lips and through our fingertips. This many and more catch our sight or feelings and find our eyes, ears, and brain. Whether we hear, see, speak, type, text, scan, sign, feel, or fax, we have word choices to make. But preachers keep watch for imbalance. We are like some other people who discern between words that are worthy and words that are demeaning. We are careful about what we say.

In the church we have a history of discerning amongst our words. Attention to good speech is summarized in the psalms, those biblical words that have been prayed regularly through Judeo-Christian history. For instance, the church's tradition of Morning Prayer begins with Psalm 51:15: "O Lord, open my lips, and my mouth will declare your praise." Here the psalmist petitions God with voice offerings instead of burnt sacrifices. And Psalm 141 is one of the appointed psalms for Evening Prayer: "Set a guard over my mouth, O LORD; keep watch over the door of my lips" (v. 3). Of all the things for which Christians could and do pray, the inherited tradition places prayer about our very own speech at the start and end our days.

John Chrysostom, a fourth-century preacher known for his use of language, describes how we can wander far from God's ways in between these times of prayer. And topping his list is not one but two references to human speech. Chrysostom reminds us how to go about our days:

> Let each one go to his affairs with fear and trembling, and so pass the time of day as one obliged to return here [to church] in the evening to give the master an account of the entire day and to ask pardon for failures. For it is impossible even if we are ten thousand times watchful to avoid being liable for all sorts of faults. Either we have said something inopportune, or have listened to idle talk, or been disturbed by some indecent thought, or have not controlled our eyes, or have spent time in vain and idle things rather than doing what we should. And that is why every evening we must ask the master's pardon for all these faults . . . then we must pass the time of night in sobriety and thus be ready to present ourselves again at the morning praise . . . [2]

Even in the fourth century, there was concern about the influence of language.

There are other psalms that depict the power of words. Two psalms in particular give us categories of harmful speech—types of speech to avoid as we make our choices:

> My companion laid hands on a friend
> and violated a covenant with me
> with speech smoother than butter,
> but with a heart set on war;
> with words that were softer than oil,
> but in fact were drawn swords. (Ps. 55:20-21)

Psalm 55 identifies what we can call *false speech*: speech that is not congruent with the speaker's real motivation. The psalmist describes a violator who speaks smoothly but whose intentions are violent. There is great discrepancy between word and deed; the deeds do not match the words. You and I know these people: they are all around us and they describe us, too. This is not a model for preaching speech, but a reminder never to speak in this manner. Instead, we want congruity between the speaker and the content of the words—we want integrity.

> My enemies are saying wicked things about me,
>> asking when I will die, and when my name will perish.
> Even if they come to see me, they speak empty words;
>> their heart collects false rumours;
>> they go outside and spread them.
> All my enemies whisper together about me
>> and devise evil against me. (Ps. 41:5-7, *Book of Common Prayer*)

Psalm 41 illustrates *slanderous speech*. The psalmist describes enemies who gossip and tell lies, whose speech is destructive. Recall your high school experiences (a sort of petri dish for this type of speech). Or think about the ubiquitous reality television shows in which we are invited to be voyeurs, watching some people prattle on about each other and gossip and tell lies in order to promote themselves. Gossip may appear light-hearted, but it always hovers at the edge of slander—words that intend to damage a person's reputation.

And there is the speech that is *outright lying*. The one lying knows the truth and chooses to create an untruth. It is a choice to persuade others to believe a falsity. It is speech that hopes to get away with something. The one lying hides the lie and so is very careful and intentional about falsifying the truth. Saint Augustine categorized lying into eight modes. Seven of these modes he says are not real lies because they were only told in order to reach a goal. But Augustine says this: "The lie which is told solely for the pleasure of lying and deceiving, that is, the real lie."[3]

We can take our cues from these psalms about good speech and harmful speech. But these days we have at least one other category of risky speech. Because these days speech is also used to create a *brand*. A brand is a product that is given superpower. And words are key to this superpower. Words tell us that a product has the power to make us younger, thinner, stronger, and wealthier. To buy that product is to buy into its world. This type of speech shapes how we shop. It is speech that has a slogan but does not necessarily follow through on its promises. The mop doesn't really soak up the spill, the diet soda isn't really nutritionally sound, and the credit card doesn't really pay for sunshine at the beach. The brand creates desire, and we want to live the life it promises. We are surrounded by slogans that promise more than they can deliver. Can we make sure that our preaching words are not perverted branding—religious packaging that lacks content? The prophet Jeremiah accuses people of this type of speech: "They have treated the wound of my people carelessly, saying, 'Peace, peace,' when there is no peace" (Jer. 8:11). Branding creates an illusion; the prophet admonishes us instead to speak truthfully about what is.

It is unlikely that any preacher or student of preaching would intentionally use harmful speech. But some might be tempted. These categories of harmful speech describe the gossip, slander, speech devoid of action, lies, and false promises that surround us every day. Preachers are human and these aspects of human language might find their way into pulpit speech. So it is important to identify these harmful forms of speech. We make a choice not to use harmful speech. It is the careless speech described by the author of James, "So also the tongue is a small member, yet it boasts of great exploits" (James 3:5). It is the speech that Jesus warns against: "I tell you, on the day of judgment you will have to give an account for every careless word you utter; for by your words you will be justified, and by your words you will be condemned" (Matt. 12:36-37). Preachers are among those who choose words carefully. We know that words are harmful and can break us. We share the work of choosing the right words.

Choosing Resurrection Speech

But preachers work to do more than simply choose the right words: we choose words that communicate resurrection speech. The resurrection appearances in the four Gospel accounts give us a place to begin.

The resurrection appearance at the end of Matthew's Gospel describes Jesus appearing to Mary Magdalene and the other Mary. Jesus greets these women. They fall at his feet and worship him. And then he instructs them not to fear but to go and tell his brothers to meet him in Galilee where he will appear to them. This part of the resurrection account is called the appearance, but it also includes Jesus' instruction to the women to "tell." In Matthew this appearance is followed by the commission to the disciples—they, too, are to go and tell. They are to use specific words as they baptize "in the name of the Father and of the Son and of the Holy Spirit" (28:19).

In the Gospel according to Luke, the women go and tell the disciples that Jesus has been raised from the dead. The two men at the tomb remind the women that Jesus had spoken of his resurrection while living. Though Jesus does not appear to the women to send them to the disciples, it is their remembering Jesus' words as they stand at the empty tomb that prompts them to return to tell the rest the news. Then there is a twist, we are told, for the apostles do not believe the women: "these words seemed to them an idle tale" (24:11). Yet this account is followed by Jesus' appearance to the disciples on the road to Emmaus. The two disciples speak with the stranger about what had happened over the last three days. And in the breaking of bread they recognize him. They recall "our hearts burning within us while he was talking to us on the road" (24:32).

In John's account Jesus appears to Mary at the site of the empty tomb. She is weeping and Jesus speaks with her, finally uttering her name. In that moment she knows him not to be the gardener but her Lord. And Jesus says to her to go and tell his brothers. She returns and announces that she has seen Jesus and relays the words he had passed on to her for their hearing.

It is the other Gospel, the other Synoptic account that does not categorically fit with these appearance narratives. In Mark, it is not Jesus but the young man at the tomb who tells Mary Magdalene, Mary the mother of James, and Salome to go and tell the disciples that Jesus will meet them in Galilee. Also, there is a command to tell of Jesus' resurrection, but in this account the women do not tell the disciples (16:8). It is key to note that this Gospel account begins not with a birth narrative but in Galilee. This is important because this is the same Galilee that is the place of promised appearance. With these words the reader has come full circle, and now the entire Gospel is a resurrection account and we are the ones who see the Lord and now go and tell.[4]

At first glance then, Christian speech, according to Scripture, is to go and tell this good news: *Jesus Christ is no longer dead but is risen.* Notice that the news is proclamatory (an announcement), it is contemporary (it is the present reality, not past news), and it is for the future (the news has repercussions). Just looking at the patterns of the four different Gospel accounts tells us some things about resurrection speech. But preachers do not simply stand up each Sunday and repeat verbatim these Gospel accounts. Reiterating Scripture is not what we mean by resurrection speech. So what is resurrection speech?

Resurrection Speech Has Particular Content

Resurrection speech in its first sense refers to the content of preachers' speech. This means that as preachers our words follow the death/life pattern that is witnessed to in the Gospel accounts. The church continues to claim that Jesus Christ has conquered death by his death and that he bestows life on us, on the whole world. God is a God of new life and by the power of the Holy Spirit, this new life is working on us and in us and through us now. It is not just new life for after-life; it is new life for our regular lives now. The church continues to profess that death is not the last word; God acts to bring about new life. We call this resurrection speech by different names. We call it gospel and we call it good news.

But new life comes out of death. Resurrection speech names both the death and the life. The church does not separate Good Friday from Easter Sunday; the cross and the empty tomb are mutually definitive. The cross tells what powers are put down by the empty tomb; the empty tomb is defined by the powers of the cross that it negates. Our preaching words follow this pattern. We name the powers that are life denying, violent, and that wield death. Resurrection speech must include both sides of the death/life pattern of the Gospel accounts.

Here are four implications of this for our preaching words:

1. ***Resurrection speech is textual because we work with the words and events of biblical texts.*** Preaching is not simply Bible study time during which we study particular texts and explore their application for our lives. The nature of preaching demands more. The texts are scrutinized for how they speak to both the power of death and God's power of new life in our midst. Sometimes the text will speak more clearly to death than to life, or vice versa. But resurrection speech is our interpretive lens and we study the text, its setting, even its rhetorical path (for example) for ways that it speaks death and life. Conversely, our resurrection speech is given particular contours because of what text/s we work with. We won't say the exact same thing about death and life each week because we work with different texts. We won't say the same thing about our needs and

the world's brokenness each week because each text points to a different aspect of loss and need and despair and to different aspects of life in the face of these deaths.

2. *Resurrection speech is contextual because it is speech shaped for particular hearers.* Preaching is not the reiteration of the biblical texts, and it is also not the reiteration of creedal statements or theological sayings. The sermon is one of the places in the order of worship where the words are intentionally dialogical—shaped by and for a particular context. There are other places during our communal worship where the repetition of certain phrases and responses has deep power. But preaching is constantly contextual. It is not just death in general of which we speak. It is not just life in general of which we speak. Preachers pay close attention to their context and the events of their surroundings (local and global) and make congruous connections between the claims of the biblical texts and what is going on that week in our hearers' midst. For example, as I write this, worldwide economic turmoil and cross-country business downsizings—or "right-sizings"—are current deaths taking their toll. What are signs of new life in the face of these deaths? We look for them. They may not be apparent yet. And we name that, too.

3. *Resurrection speech must pass the "So what?" test.* Preaching speech does not mean that the preacher uses scriptural or theological sayings as a slogan, as if invoking a biblical word or making a theological point fixes everything. Resurrection speech, preaching that deals honestly with our needs and wounds and deaths and death-dealing ways, will not give way to an easy fix. We do not toss off an easy "Jesus heals" saying or a simple "God rescues us" pronouncement. When preachers find the good news words arising from a particular text we make sure we wrestle with them. We make sure they can stand the "So what?" or the "How does this make a difference?" test.[5]

4. *Resurrection speech shapes us for resurrection life.* There are three insights related to this statement. First, the death/life pattern is central to a whole constellation of related patterns. You recognize the words: justice, mercy, righteousness, love, community, faithfulness, wholeness, grace. Second, resurrection speech does not send us to relax on the couch all day but intends to shape us for a life of service. It is not speech intended

to secure our individual borders, though it bears that fruit, but is for each of us as a member in the whole body of Christ. And third, it is speech that shapes us for life now, not simply life after death. Today we are made new. Today we are members of Christ's body—signs of God's love in the world. This speech shapes us to live life according to its life-giving pattern.

Resurrection Speech Has Particular Effects

I have been describing resurrection speech, its definition, and the contours of its content. But here is a second meaning of resurrection speech for preaching: it is speech that causes us to see and live in the world in a new way. We want preaching to change lives and change the world. We want not only to see what is tangible but also to see what is possible. In order to do this we work with words in a particular way. This book is about language but is also about a specific type of language: *imagery.*

Imagery is the type of speech that elicits an experiential connection, a sensory memory, or recognition. We can use it interchangeably with *evocative language,* which is the umbrella that has gathered under it metaphors, similes, personification, analogy, synecdoche, allusion, metonymy, and even stories and illustrations. Preachers use imagery in a fashion similar to poetry:

> Poetry is not simply communicating information, though that may be entailed. Poetry happens when two realities are compared in such a way that an ethos shift occurs. As is frequently the case, the poet of Amherst puts the matter best. She sees that some realities are so large, some mysteries so deep, that they can only be told slant.[6]

Imagery is the type of language used to tell things slant.

Here are some preliminary things to know about imagery as we begin our study of evocative language in the pulpit:

1. *Imagery is necessary and is different than informational language.*

Informational language is language that tells us who, what, where, when, and how by the use of straightforward terms. We call 911 to report a traffic accident, and we must give as many of these details as precisely as possible. We use language to convey facts and details. Imagery, instead, is about connecting to memory, feelings, and life experiences. It is language that evokes emotion and aesthetic response. It is the type of language we reach for because we know the "magnitude and particularity of the subject defy description."[7] Imagery, compared to informational language, is not a lesser form of language but is a different form of language. We now know it even forms in our brains differently. One author, writing about neurological discoveries concerning the use of language, makes this distinction: "There is stylistic importance of logical argument and testability in science. Literature is often trying to prove something too, but characteristically convinces us by evocation of emotion and aesthetic response—limbic functions—along the lines of Keats's 'Beauty is truth, truth is beauty.'"[8]

2. *Imagery is specific and is different from abstract, conceptual language.* Abstract language includes words like grace, salvation, forgiveness, sin, and redemption. These may be the vocabulary words of the church from biblical texts, prayers, and hymnody, but they are large concepts. Justice, love, freedom, hunger, war, and trauma are more examples of abstract conceptual words. Imagery strives to show what these concepts look like in our lives so that we connect with their realities. Freedom, this morning, looked like a Muslim woman in a blue headscarf in Urumqi, China, as she denounced communist rule in that country's far western region and rallied people to join her shouts of protest against regional government beatings and deaths.

3. *Imagery is evocative and is different from denotative understandings of language.* Denotative use of words focuses on dictionary definitions or original meanings. Imagery may be used to show us what these denotative meanings look like. But more often imagery is connotative—it is less concerned with our recollection of an exact meaning of a word and more interested in connecting us to the lived-out meanings of the word. A dog may be a four-footed creature that belongs to genus *canine*, but I will think of Inky, the Black Labrador/Irish Setter mix who let two elementary school-age sisters snuggle him like a pillow.

Imagery is not optional for preaching. It is not an additive to conceptual or theoretical writing. It is how our minds work to make sense of life. We are hardwired for evocative language. In chapter 3 there are lists of long-term practices for growing our evocative linguistic capacities, as well as exercises for the weekly work of sermon preparation to strengthen use of images in sermons.

Before I turn to those practices, however, we will take one more step back for another expansive view of language. This time, in chapter 2, I will take up the question of what our words do in sermons with an overview of contemporary theories of language.

For Further Reading

Brueggemann, Walter. *Finally Comes the Poet: Daring Speech for Proclamation.* Minneapolis: Fortress Press, 1989. The acclaimed Hebrew Bible scholar invites preachers to the land of poetic speech.

Frankfurt, Harry G. *On Bullshit.* Princeton: Princeton University Press, 2005. Frankfurt approaches the topic in order to develop a theory of its existence and to investigate its ongoing presence in human speech.

Hilkert, Mary Catherine. *Naming Grace: Preaching and the Sacramental Imagination.* New York: Continuum, 1997. Hilkert approaches preaching as the opportunity to build our imaginations and tune us to see God at work in our midst.

Lischer, Richard. *The End of Words: The Language of Reconciliation in a Culture of Violence.* Grand Rapids: Eerdmans, 2005. This book is the published collection of Lischer's Lyman Beecher Lectures in Preaching at Yale Divinity School. Lischer looks at the overabundance of words in the world and challenges the words we use for preaching.

McEntyre, Marilyn Chandler. *Caring for Words in a Culture of Lies.* Grand Rapids: Eerdmans, 2009. This is another text that analyzes word use in contemporary cultures. McEntyre issues an urgent call for our precise and caring use of words.

Taylor, Barbara Brown. *When God is Silent.* Boston: Cowley, 1998. In her 1997 series of lectures for the Lyman Beecher Lectures in Preaching at Yale Divinity School, Taylor evokes the need for words that speak to truth. She names our hunger for real words, our overuse of words, and the need for our restraint with words.

Chapter 2

What Preaching Words Do

A part of language and imagery work is to look carefully at how we use words. What do we think happens when we speak the words of the sermon? Are the meanings of the words immediately known and shared by all the listeners? In order to answer these and a few other questions about the use of words this chapter will describe some of the ways theorists think about how language makes meaning. We have considered how preachers are like all other humans—we communicate. And that preachers are also like some other humans—we are careful about the words we use. We have also thought about preachers as a unique group—we choose certain words to proclaim good news. Now we will look at several ways that preachers work with words.

This chapter provides a general introduction to some ways that scholars classify theories of language. Theories are helpful because they organize and analyze our experience and extend our knowledge. We will look at six different theories of language. These categories will help you reflect on your understanding of the power of language in sermons: Which category best describes how you use words? Which categories present new ideas to you about language? What do you want to do differently as a result of reading these categories? As you read through this section you should begin to identify other questions about the function of language in sermons.

1. Preaching Communicates
This is an obvious category. Preaching communicates. The preacher identifies what she wants to put into words, finds the words, and says them so

that the congregation can hear them. This is an old pattern of communication: message, sender, and receiver. Let's say we want to communicate resurrection life. We identify the words we will use to describe resurrection life: we describe it biblically or doctrinally or point to life examples that give a picture of what we mean by resurrection life. Then we say these things in the sermon and expect that the listeners will receive this message about resurrection life. According to this model of communication the only things that get in the way of the message being sent and received are unclear speech, ambient noise, lack of volume, unfamiliar vocabulary, and interruptions. Our preaching work is to identify what we intend to communicate and to say it clearly. We may use examples or stories to assist the communication, but the main focus is that the content of the message is sent and received.

There are different ideas about communication within the field of communication studies. What I describe above is an *objective theory model*. This type of approach to language asserts that there is a cause-and-effect relationship between the thing said and the thing heard. And the better we understand the tool of language and what different language choices mean, the more effective choices we will make as communicators. According to this model, the language of the sermon should clearly convey the message of the sermon.

But the objective theory model is at one end of a continuum of language theories within communication studies. At the other end of the continuum are the *interpretive theories of communication*. These theories see more complexity in the act of communication. These models emphasize subjective personal experience and perception as key to determining how messages are received. The receiver does not automatically receive the message being sent. Instead, these theories say that the transmission of a message is a complex act because the meaning is negotiated between sender and receiver. Senders and receivers create, sustain, experience, interpret, work toward mutual understanding, and challenge language structures. To continue with our example: preaching that communicates resurrection life according to interpretive theories of communication will not follow a sender-receiver pattern. The preacher does not simply determine how to present the message of resurrection life that is to be received by the hearers. Instead, the preacher knows that the meaning of language about resurrection life only exists within first-person experience and interpretation of events. The work of preaching, then, is to initiate shared reflection on how we have experienced resurrection life and how we have interpreted the biblical, doctrinal, and experiential claims about it. The preacher cannot provide a fixed meaning of resurrection life that is to be sent and received by the listeners. The preacher is instead initiating discourse, and the listener will make the connections and fill in what is needed to make meaning.

Of course, there are middle-of-the-road communication theories. All theories overlap, and this overlap is true for communication theories, too. These middle-ground models say that we can identify the thing that needs to be communicated and that we can also take into consideration the experiences and perceptions of the listeners. According to these middle-ground models, a sermon on resurrection life will assert a particular understanding of this focus even as the sermon acknowledges a variety of perceived meanings. These models honor multiple interpretations but also understand the preacher's power to change those interpretations rather than only exist alongside them.

Questions:
- As a preacher are you able to make your sermon clearly understood by every listener?
- Do you think of preaching as adding a suggestion or observation to the listeners' individual and shared experience of the particular sermonic theme?
- Do preachers set out a theme or experience and trust the listeners to make the connections in order for the sermon to be meaningful?

2. Preaching Persuades

This is a venerable and foundational model for speaking about the purpose of words in preaching. According to this theory of language, words are to be selected and arranged in order to persuade the listeners to the preacher's intended goal. This model has centuries of influence on preaching. Sometimes preaching has been defined synonymously with *rhetoric*. For that reason we will first look at the history of persuasive speech before we look at the ways it is understood as a model of language use for contemporary work in preaching.

The Greek philosopher Aristotle (384–322 B.C.E.) defined rhetoric as "the faculty of discovering in the particular case what are the available means of persuasion."[1] In other words, rhetoricians study what types of communication work best to convince particular audiences to think and act in specific ways. Aristotle categorized three means or proofs for persuasive speech: *ethos* (the credibility or character of the speaker); *logos* (the logical proof, the use of evidence and arguments in a speech); and *pathos* (the emotional appeal). These three means deal with the substance of a speech, its arrangement, and the character of the speaker. Aristotle employed rhetoric as the way for a society to make practical decisions. Rhetoric was not, as in the view of his teacher Plato, used in the quest of philosophical truths but was for the ordinary citizen. Aristotle was determined to help the common citizen (at that time, a land-owning male) participate in public life in a time when there were no professional attorneys. Although the Sophists, teachers of public speech, were a resource for many citizens, Aristotle thought they were too focused on the judicial system and neglected the other contexts of public speech (travel, ceremonial speech, government legislature). His system of rhetoric was designed to help the regular citizen claim personal rights and to help all citizens argue for the good of their common life.

Cicero (106–43 B.C.E.) was a Latin rhetorician who, in his work *De Inventione*, expanded Aristotelian rhetoric into a fivefold method: *invention* (determine what should be said to make one's case); *arrangement* (the outline, progression of thought); *elocution* (figures of speech and sound to make one's case, style); *memory* (delivery preparations); and *delivery*. He further delineated the orator's *duties* into three categories: to instruct, to delight, and to persuade. Each duty is connected with a level of *style*: plain for proving, middle for delight or pleasure, and grand for persuasion or moving.[2]

While early preaching to a great extent followed the Jewish synagogue model of exposition of sacred texts, the Greek and Latin rhetorical tradition exerted enormous influence on the church. Augustine of Hippo (354–430 B.C.E.) was a teacher of rhetoric and was especially influenced by Cicero's works. He believed that Christians should make use of rhetoric and expressed this ideal in what is usually considered the first Christian work in homiletics, *De Doctrina Christiana*. Many persons in his time were suspicious of rhetoric, believing it to be a verbal skill pagans employed to attack Christianity, but Augustine argued that Christian purposes were strengthened by the use of rhetoric.

The ancients introduced these methods and duties of speech to describe and prescribe the function of language. These concepts were used in the late Middle Ages and later in the Renaissance, Reformation, and Romantic periods. By the eighteenth century public-speaking courses were known as elocution courses, and in each century since then a major book on rhetoric has influenced preachers.[3] Some homileticians describe the early years of Christian preaching as Christianized rhetoric.

The debate about the place and primacy of rhetoric in relation to preaching is ongoing. Some contemporary homileticians distrust an emphasis on rhetoric. To employ rhetoric, they say, is to depend on human efforts to form a sermon into the word of God. A sermon on resurrection life will be an effective sermon if the preacher is faithful to the interpretation of the biblical text and brings theological acumen to the act of interpretation. Other homileticians claim that all intentional speech is a rhetorical act. As long as we structure our discourse, we are using rhetoric. It is the pool we humans swim in and is most certainly our preaching pool. The preacher who prepares a sermon on resurrection life will think through many different ways to make that sermon persuasive, for example: the best structure of the sermon, stories about resurrection life that will connect to that congregation, and the sermon's length. A middle-ground position about the preacher's use of rhetoric is to say that humans have the power and freedom to shape speech so it is best to use this responsibly and with humility.

Not only is the relationship between rhetoric and homiletics complicated and even contested, rhetorical theory on its own is a diverse discipline. In early rhetorical theory, language is the vehicle for persuasive communication. Language is a controllable tool, a medium for the message. The speaker's understanding of the audience and persuasive intention governs the use of language. Some rhetorical theorists now understand language as a human construct, creating rather than referring to reality. Rhetorical theory includes multiple views of the function of language.

This volume claims that preachers use rhetorical methods continuously. Some of these ways include congregational analysis, choice of stories and illustrations, choices about the tone of the sermon, word choice, sermon form, even sermon length. This is a middle-ground approach—we cannot make our sermons be the word of God, but we put our best efforts forth in service of God's agency in and through our words. A sermon on resurrection life will identify a sermon focus and be carefully prepared according to the dynamics of ethos, logos, and pathos.

Questions:
- How does preaching differ from other instances of rhetoric in the twenty-first century?

- Does a rhetorically well-prepared sermon ensure an effective sermon?
- What are your responsibilities as one who has rhetorical power?

3. Preaching Tells the Truth

Some preachers understand that the purpose of a sermon is to tell the truth about God and all aspects of the Christian life. We will again look at a historical timeline to understand this theory of language. In the eighteenth century there were specific movements in the history of philosophical ideas that influenced thinking about the function of language. Two of these movements were *empiricism* and *rationalism*. Although these positions about how we know things (epistemology) appeared before the eighteenth century, they came to the forefront by this time. The Enlightenment period in continental Europe was marked by a concern for reason as the source of knowledge. Emphasis on reason demarcated the Enlightenment from the Middle Ages (a time of tradition, irrationalism, and superstition). Empiricism emphasizes knowledge through verifiable personal experience. All ideas come to us through our five senses, it says, which can be tested. We know things through evidence and experiments. Rationalism emphasizes knowledge that comes from reasoning, from logical extrapolation. All things are dependent on first principles, general rules that govern the way the world works. We simply deduce or extrapolate what follows from these first laws to say how things are and will be in life.

Sermons that most clearly illustrate the use of the rationalism-Enlightenment characteristics are those that follow a deductive form, positing a general truth and showing how all things proceed from that truth. Logic is favored over pathos or ethos. A sermon on resurrection life would be structured in order to prove how this theme is reasonable, logical, and therefore applicable to our lives. Sermons that best exemplify the empirical-Enlightenment model of language are characterized by a focus on what has proved knowable (verifiable) over time. A sermon on resurrection life would define this term and then stress ways that we can know it through personal experiences. It is true because we can verify it by our senses.

Language, according to these models, is a vehicle for communicating what is known to be true. Our preaching language is able to depict what is real about God. Our language is able to prove these claims either through logic or through the test of human experience. According to these models preachers are able to determine what they say and what is heard; the preacher's meaning clearly carries through in the communication process.

Questions:
- Is the preacher the one who has the truth to tell?
- Are sermons meaningful because they are primarily logical?
- Does a sermon's claim need to be empirically verifiable to be true?
- Should we preach from texts that seem illogical or unverifiable?

4. Preaching Gives Us a Language

Some preachers think of sermons as the means by which congregations are immersed in the narratives of the biblical story and Christian tradition. This view of sermons is related to the theory of language known as *structuralism*. This understanding of language came about in reaction to the empirical and rationalist models of language and meaning described above. According to this view, meaning is not lodged within individual's understanding of axioms or verifiable, repeatable, sensory experiences; rather, meaning comes through the *structures* that define and permeate our ways of acting and knowing. None of us makes ourselves on our own; we are shaped (at least) by psychological, sociological, and linguistic structures. We inhabit these structures. I see a person in a hospital wearing a white, knee-length coat and I think "doctor." My label comes out of a shared structure for giving a white-coated person in this setting this name. In another setting a white-coated person may be a dentist or a butcher. But the language system enables this identification. Our language systems build the very structures that perpetuate and continually shape our worldviews and values. Anything that we say simply represents the deeper ongoing structure of which we are a part.

Sermons influenced by structuralism do not focus on what the biblical author intended in a given text or on finding the original kernel of truth from a text. Rather, the sermon's focus comes from analyzing the text itself—its patterns and structures—to get at meaning. Preachers trust that the text makes a present-day claim on us and that it is to be encountered repeatedly for a fresh claim. Our system of signs (our structure) encounters the text's structure. For some preachers this means that the purpose of the sermon is to relanguage listeners. The hearers are to be shaped according to the structure of the biblical story and canon or the church's confessions and traditions or according to a particular congregation. Preaching shows that the world of language for Christians is a different world than the secular world and is a particular way of living in the world. A sermon would focus on resurrection life because that theme was identified as a structure of a particular passage and resonates with the deep structure of the canon. The sermon would show how this focus arises from the text and shapes our contemporary worldview.

Questions:
- What structures affect our views of the world?
- How can we recognize the structures we live amidst?
- Is the purpose of preaching to relanguage us?

5. Preaching Interrupts

It may seem strange to think about preaching as an activity that interrupts other activities. We are more aware of those things that interrupt preaching like a siren, a baby's cry, or a candy wrapper. But some preachers not only think about the structures that shape our realities but how these structures ought to be named, challenged, and interrupted. While we may label this approach to preaching "prophetic preaching," there is a theory of language that supports this exacting way of examining the language of texts. Preachers borrow from *deconstructionists* when they look for the embedded biases, power structures, and cultural conditioning of texts. In particular this deconstructive work happens when preachers identify the binary systems present in the text(s). Binary pairs are two terms that exist in relation to each other. And instead of assuming that one term is privileged over the other, we look to see how each term is actually a part of the other. Day needs night for its definition; in the same way, night needs day, and we scrutinize these terms to examine how we privilege one over the other and what that linguistic hierarchy means for us. We look at structures like class, race, and gender and scrutinize how one term in a relationship became privileged over the other.

Sermons that use deconstructionist methods show that the preacher has studied the text(s) using these methods. The sermon itself may be an exploration of textual terms, unfolding biases and power structures, and show how terms are not fixed as polar opposites. Preaching proceeds from a place of respect for plurality, a deconstruction of systems that privilege certain groups, and recognition of the relativity of truth-claims. A sermon on resurrection life will have looked closely at resurrection—what is it paired with? We cannot speak of life apart from death, nor of death apart from life. A sermon on resurrection life will consider these sorts of language claims and how this careful deconstructive work enlarges our concept of resurrection.

Questions:
- Are there power dynamics in every biblical text?
- Is it important to look for binary pairs in biblical text(s)?
- How can this way of reading texts help sermon effectiveness?

6. Preaching Transforms

Another theory of language focuses on the central question of this chapter: What does preaching do? *Performative* theories of language claim that words perform the actions to which they refer. Words, according to this theory, do not simply make a statement, give information, make emotional connections, or persuade us. Words actually *do* the thing that is spoken. A classic example of this is the declaration "I do" during a wedding ceremony. These words do not refer to a marriage, give report of it, or describe the action. The words do the action. They are the vehicle of the act. They are the way that the action happens. Another example is a musical score, which is realized only in the risks of the performance. Meaning not only precedes the act but emerges in the performance. According to this theory, words are world making. Words transform us and bring into being the things that they name.

Preachers that understand language as performative utterance believe that a sermon is an event. It is an event because the sermon's language causes something to happen in the experience of the hearers. A sermon causes a new thing in our lives. A sermon makes something happen. A sermon on resurrection life still comes from the work of biblical exegesis, doctrinal scrutiny, evaluation of context, and so forth. But the preacher knows that the sermon is shaped so that hearers encounter resurrection—so that something happens. The word is a deed and in its utterance something changes or begins.

Questions:
- What are other examples of ways that words perform actions?

- How is your responsibility as a preacher different according to this theory of language?
- What would you like your preaching to perform?

These are macro views of preaching that have repercussions for micro choices about the language of our sermons. Work through the questions. Consider the language theory of sermons that have shaped you. You may resonate with more than one theory of language because, while some categories are in conflict with each other, some categories can be seen as complimentary. You may find affinity with rhetoric and performance theories. Or with rhetoric and empirical theories. Begin to identify why these theories attract you. From that vantage point you can begin to critique and borrow from other communication approaches. And roll up your sleeves because now we will walk through a week's worth of sermon preparation work while we pay close attention to language and imagery issues.

For Further Reading

Allen, O. Wesley. *The Homiletic of All Believers: A Conversational Approach.* Louisville: Westminster John Knox, 2005. Allen works with the metaphor of conversation to identify the nature and purpose of preaching and Christian life. This postmodern homiletic takes seriously the nature of our language structures in the ongoing life of the church.

Childers, Jana, ed. *Purposes of Preaching.* St. Louis: Chalice, 2004. This edited volume is a collection of ten homileticians' writings about the nature and purpose of the act of preaching. The ideas are varied and provocative.

Craddock, Fred B. *As One Without Authority.* (Nashville: Abingdon, 1971). This is the watershed book of the New Homiletic. Craddock, influenced by the work of Søren Kierkegaard, presents an alternative homiletic to the proposition-focused sermons.

Hogan, Lucy Lind, and Robert Reid. *Connecting with the Congregation: Rhetoric and the Art of Preaching.* Nashville: Abingdon, 1999. Hogan and Reid provide a review of the principles of rhetoric and revisit the ways that preaching relates to rhetoric.

Lose, David J. *Confessing Jesus Christ: Preaching in a Postmodern World.* Grand Rapids: Eerdmans, 2003. Lose presents a postmodern homiletic while providing summaries and critiques of concurrent homiletical theories.

McClure, John S. *Otherwise Preaching: A Postmodern Ethic for Homiletics.* St. Louis: Chalice, 2001. McClure works with the theories of Emmanuel Levinas and language to speak about the tasks of preaching.

Chapter 3

Weekly Word Work

In chapter 1 we looked at the ways that preaching words are important. Preachers choose the words that will become preaching speech or, as we called it, resurrection speech. And we looked at the ways that words do this—not just through their content but also by their effect on us. Words have the power to name what is and to create a glimpse of what can be possible. Imagery, in particular, evokes our connection to the sermonic claim because we relate our experience, our memories, and our emotions to the subject matter at hand. I can read the news about the state of public education and think through issues of learning and access. But public education takes on a different level of meaning when I think about my sister's advocacy work for students with parents, schools, and communities.

In chapter 2 we reviewed theories about the power of our preaching words. Some of the theories, like communication theories and rhetorical theories, are more familiar to us. Other theories may be recognizable but less familiar. Yet they are new ways that we can think about the power of words in sermons. Each one of these theories raises questions for reflection. And together they raise questions about our goals for our preaching words: What do we think our words have the power to do? What do we want our words to do?

In this chapter we will focus on sermon preparation work. Language is necessary for preaching, and imagery is a primary form of sermonic language. Here we will look at steps we can follow during sermon preparation to attend to language and imagery in sermons, in particular, the following:

- Interpreting for words and imagery

- Imagining words and imagery

- Writing words and imagery

- Preparing the manuscript with words and images

- Editing words and images

- Planning for long-term work with words and images

Some new preachers are surprised by the amount of work that goes on in preparation for preaching. And some preachers think that too much preparation somehow detracts from the power of the sermon. But we can reconsider this claim. James Forbes, in his Lyman Beecher Lectures on preaching, says this about sermon preparation:

> After stressing the importance of the anointing of the Spirit, someone once responded as if I were suggesting that we can be relieved of the rigor and tedium of sermon preparation. "Oh, I just want to thank you for telling us about the anointing of the Spirit. You know, I have always felt that the hard labor of traditional homiletical rules was more than necessary. . . . Thank you for showing us how to preach without all that unnecessary toil."
>
> I usually respond to such comments by finding a tactful way of declining the gratitude and explaining that I do not believe the anointing of the Holy Spirit relieves us from the responsibility of thoughtful diligence in exchange for magical toil-free preparation. If we need a proof-text, a better choice would be Luke 11:42c: "these you ought to have done, without neglecting the others."[1]

Let's hold responsibility and inspiration in tension. And let's think a bit more about the relationship of the sermon preparation process and the preaching event.

The Sermon Process: Twice-Born Words

Preachers prepare for sermons in different ways. Some preachers work on several sermons at a time, well in advance of the preaching time. Others schedule retreat time away from regular workdays in order to plan a part of the year or a year's worth of sermons. Some are members of preaching groups and travel in order to meet with others to do this sort of planning. These communal retreats serve to renew and expand their preaching lives. Other preachers meet with local ministerium groups once a month or more, or less often. But many preachers work on sermons by a week-to-week schedule. Scheduling exigencies arise and days off are planned but the sermon preparation must still fit into the week's hours. This chapter focuses on the ways that the preacher works with language during the time of sermon preparation. The one-week timeline is the ruling framework here, but this week's work with words is adaptable to any of the time frames mentioned.

Our work on sermons is like our work in many other areas of life: it is work in the present time that is shaped according to a future event. It is, in some ways, like the food shopping done in order to prepare for a festive family meal. It is like pruning winter vines for summer flowers. It is like running hills, miles, and sprints for marathon training. The end event defines the nature and scope of the present-tense work. If I want this particular meal, these flowers, or the finish line at this marathon I will do these specific preparations. The end event of a week's sermon work—or of the longer-term work of sermon planning—is the same: the preaching event. For preachers, the future event of preaching defines a certain framework for our preparations.

This is obvious, of course. Many of these dynamics are introduced and examined by other books, including those in the Elements of Preaching series. Here are a few of those dynamics: our sermon preparation is shaped by identifying who will be in the congregation; by identifying what the preaching context will be (Sunday gathering, nursing home, midweek service); by identifying the sermon's texts, rhetorical needs, place among global events, and mode of proclamation.

However, the topic of this book is the language of the sermon and the focus is on crafting that language for the sermon as a spoken event. Here, we will specifically think about the sermon as an event of orality and aurality—of speaking and of hearing—and explore what this claim about the future event means for sermonic language in our preparations.

To understand the sermon as an oral/aural event means that our week's work is not done once the sermon is "written." Our week's work is never finished ahead of the preaching event. Our work reaches its key place and fullness in the proclamation event itself—in the liturgy, the worship service, among the people. The proclamation will, of course, continue through our hearing and our actions out into the world, but the focal moment is the preaching event. During the week we can easily get caught up thinking otherwise. We see our words lined up, all moving left to right, and we reach our four-single-spaced-pages goal, but this written form is not the same thing as the sermon. We casually say on Thursday, "I need to finish my sermon for Sunday," or "I can go out to dinner Saturday because my sermon is done." We use the language of completion. But completion at this point is only proleptic of Sunday morning worship. Our present-tense work serves the future event. It leans toward it. Even the full manuscript rehearsed many times is not the done deal.

To say the sermon is an oral/aural event means that we have a great discrepancy before us. The future event is an oral/auditory event, but the preparation is not done in these modes. Cellists prepare for auditions and concerts by practicing cello. Race-car drivers prepare with particular cars and selected tracks. Systems analysts categorize data according to the needs of specific computer programs and functions. But this correlation between mode of preparation and mode of performance is not the norm for sermon preparation. Instead, preachers prepare for the oral/aural event by reading, writing, inward contemplation, and consultation with other preachers. Preachers prepare by hearing world news, reading blogs and sermon Web sites, consulting books, and translating texts. Preachers prepare by visiting art museums, watching movies, listening to music. Preachers prepare through their engagement with all of the regular pastoral activities of a week. Some preachers, inspired by newer homiletical insights, do read Scripture aloud and rehearse sermons orally. A few preachers even prepare sermons orally, speaking phrases and sentences and whole paragraphs aloud in order to check the focus of the sermon and envision—by hearing—what should come next. But overall the modes of preparation—reading, reflection, and writing—are different from the normative mode of preaching: speaking and hearing.

And yet this is not to say that preparation and preaching event are not inextricably related. One serves the other; indeed, one cannot exist without the other. Preparation is penultimate to the event and the event occurs on the shoulders of preparation. Theologian Dietrich Bonhoeffer placed the two activities in even closer relationship: "A sermon must be twice-born, once in the study and once in the pulpit."[2] This claim goes beyond noticing congruency between our preparations and the preaching event. "Twice-born" puts weight to our preparatory work. Our efforts in preparation are to be so serious that they bring about birth in our "study." With this in mind we will look at the ways in which sermon preparation time includes work on words and imagery. We begin with exegesis.

Interpreting for Words and Imagery

Exegesis means "to lead out." Exegesis is the work we do with a biblical text in order to interpret it. Over the years biblical scholars have formalized several approaches to biblical exegesis in order for meaning to be led out of the biblical texts and into our lives: historical criticism, form criticism, literary criticism, and the like. There are many other exegetical methods, and these are described elsewhere in this series (and in other books as well).[3] Yet one aspect of exegesis has changed over time and is important to note here. Years ago interpreters imagined that they could study a passage with historical methods, clearly identify the meaning of the passage, and then explain or interpret it for present-day listeners. Now interpreters understand that our exegetical work is more interactive than surgical in nature. A proper method will not enable us to extract the proper interpretation. There are multiple interpretations of texts, and who one is as an interpreter shapes one's interpretations of the texts.

In general, exegesis is the time for us to ask questions of the text, put on our detective eyewear, and let the conversation with the text begin. Preachers often start with prayer, and then identify the parameters of the text for the sermon. Some preachers read the passage aloud and then begin to list their questions and observations. Others look at the text and list these queries and ideas. Preachers make use of various exegetical methods in order to: study the passage in its original language; identify what can be known about the historical, sociological, and economic setting of the text; identify the text according to literary genre, rhetorical form, and canonical placement and function; think about the connections between the text's world and our context. There are other aspects of the text to investigate, too. Some preachers ask questions about God's activity in and through the text at this point. Some exegetes identify theological doctrines closely related to the text. Some study the history of interpretation of the text and ideologies associated with the text. This work is done with an eye toward the preacher's context and current local, national, and global events.

All of this describes a rudimentary exegetical outline for preachers. But our interest is in the ways that exegetical work helps us choose words and imagery for the sermon. As you study the setting of the text or review language issues or identify the text's literary genre you can simultaneously attend to the language and imagery of the text. Here are five ways that you can attend to words and imagery concurrent with the other exegetical steps named above.

1. **Study the Words and Images in the Text.** This sounds obvious. After all, many preachers have studied the original languages or have learned how to use language tools in order to translate meanings of words, and the importance of word tense and syntax. But sometimes exegetes will rush to get to theological meaning or a historical insight and pass over the words and images. Instead: slow down. Look up the word *temple* again even if you think you have a working knowledge of its definition according to that particular passage. It is a word with various definitions and it is most likely used as an image in the text where it appears. Look up the history of meanings of the word.

And pay attention to verbs, too. For instance, investigate what it means that Mark's account of the baptism of Jesus uses a word (Greek *eis*) for the descent of the Spirit that means "into" or "in" instead of "upon" (Mark 1:10). In other words, go slowly through the text, word by word, early in the exegetical stage of sermon preparation. Look at the original languages or compare translations. See what words are translated differently in the comparative versions. Ask yourself why they are translated differently and what the degrees of difference may mean. Notice syntax and verb tense and what those choices mean for interpreting the text. Spend time with these words because they could be a goldmine for the sermon.

2. **Keep Notes about Important Words.** Exegetes study and take notes on historical information, theological questions, and a myriad of other textual discoveries and insights. And it is just as important to keep notes about key words. This is because a word could become the focus of the sermon. To use our example from above, the idea of "temple" could become the sermon focus. A temple is a place or building signifying the presence of God and is a place of worship. But temple in the biblical canon has multiple meanings. For instance, a temple is a building; Scripture describes several of them from different historical periods, Jesus says he

is the Temple, and Paul says our bodies are each a temple of the Holy Spirit. "Temple" now becomes an image layered with meanings. What does our passage mean by the word *temple*? Study the words of the passage, write down what you discover, and keep all of these notes. Find a way to file them for future work on the same passage. This groundwork can be used more than once. It may be that when you get to the end of your exegetical work that you find one word translation or verb tense is an accurate summary of the whole sermon focus. So keep notes about the words and images.

3. ***Write Down Images That Come to Mind.*** When you first read the text, whether silently or aloud, you will already make connections to the text. You will remember if you have studied it before, preached from it before, or thought about any aspect of it before. Our minds make connections, so do not be surprised if you immediately experience associations with the text. Keep track of these associations. These associations come in many imagery forms: stories, examples, and metaphors are all examples of imagery associations. You may associate a movie scene with a part of the text. Or a word may remind you of a poem or a passage in a novel. You may read an image in the text and picture a contemporary example in your mind. Write down all of these imagery associations. This is not to say that you will use them in the sermon. You may discard all of them. But, then again, maybe you won't. Or maybe they will lead to another image later in the preparation process. I've learned to trust this process: write down stories, quotes, examples, or other images that come to mind even if they seem unconnected to the text. You will have plenty of time to continue exegetical work and double check your interpretive claims. For now, trust your intuitive instincts and write down these associations.

4. ***Write Down Words, Sentences, or Sentence Fragments That Come to Mind.*** Just as your mind will make imagistic associations, so also your mind will work on analyzing and synthesizing the exegetical ideas. And sometimes you will think of a word or a brief phrase that seems important for the focus of the sermon. Write these thoughts down even though you may not know the sermon focus yet. Eventually these snippets of words can come to mind sounding like they will sound in the sermon—already formed as proclamatory speech rather than study notes. In other words, you may hear yourself preach portions of the sermon in your mind while

you are still in the preparation process. Write down any words or phrases or sentences that come to mind. Again, all of these word associations will be checked for theological strength and textual accountability throughout the sermon preparation process. But this is another way that your mind works on the sermon so keep track of those inspirational words.

5. ***Begin to Categorize the Words and Images.*** So far we have thought about the exegetical process and paid attention to words and images in the text and in our creative associations. Here is a next step: begin to categorize these notable words and images. These categories serve as a way to organize your notes about words and images and cause you to think about why these words or images seem important in the exegetical process. I think of three categories, though you may think of more. One category is *Summary Words and Images.* These are key words and images that you believe hold the focus point of the passage. Another category is *Hinge Words and Images.* This is the category for words or images that seem, at first glance, to mean one thing but instead, through exegetical discovery, mean something else. They can then become a hinge or turning point in the sermon—a time of discovery or deeper association. Finally, there is the category of *Descriptive Words and Images.* These words and images do not function as summaries of the sermon focus or as hinges for key points during the sermon. Instead, they are words and images that function as examples of a part of the sermon. They relate to one aspect of the sermon but are not key words or images that sustain the focus of the whole sermon.

As with any exegetical practice, practice breeds familiarity. Arrange your exegetical work so that you include these steps and eventually they will become an intuitive and natural part of your sermon preparation process.

Imagining Words and Imagery

When we preach we do more than repeat the words of the biblical text. So while preachers pay attention to words and imagery during exegetical work, we also work to understand what the textual words and images mean for us in our time. We work to see what it means for us to live by those words and images because we value the ways that they speak of God, the world, and humanity. At this point in the sermon preparation process we not only study to see what textual words and images mean, we permit our minds to make new associations in relation to these words and images. For instance, we can do exegetical research to find out what "living water" meant in biblical times, but we also want to shape our language about this water: What did it mean for the Samaritan woman and what it is for our lives? I let my imagination wander and I think about sand, dust, tan colors, sun that makes you squint, quiet (because other people are resting midday), how much distance to the village well and the size of her water container. Or I'll start thinking about the well and the water. Maybe one of my imaginings will take over. Homiletician Linda Clader says it this way:

> We may have been pouring over erudite commentaries, aware only of our most rational function, and—bam!—we feel the truth of the scriptural story in our hearts and in our bones. Neurologists tell us that our limbic system, our "emotional brain," behaves "something like a valve, deciding what will grab our attention and what will not." They call this phenomenon "salience"—that which jumps out at you.[4]

Our goal is to work with the textual words and images and to find our own words and images for each sermon. This is faithful work because to shape appropriate new words in order to expand on textual words and imagery is incarnational work: we are tethered by the biblical text but work to show its gospel meanings for our lives now.[5] Here are some practical suggestions for going about this work during your sermon preparation process.

1. **Listen.** What a strange place to begin—listening in order to write toward the speech-act of preaching. But it is a way to observe, to scrutinize. As Natalie Goldberg writes, "Listening is receptivity. The deeper you can listen, the better you can write. You take in the way things are without judgment, and the next day you can write the truth about the way things are."[6] It is deep attention. Listen to the biblical text, to your questions, to your preconceived notions. Listen to the connections you make to the world, to your community of faith. Listen to the people who will listen to you, listen to the world in this week, toward the preaching day. It will include some literal listening, but a preacher's listening involves a great deal of imaginative, empathic attentiveness to what is all around you.

2. **Make Notes.** Some preachers still carry a bound notebook, pocket size or larger, and write down any and all ideas that might influence or end up

in a sermon. Making notes is an alternative to the preacher's notebook. Any form of paper and writing implement will do: when you are listening deeply and see something, when the spark comes, when the unconscious mind sets something down alongside the passage you are carrying about, type it into your PDA or write it down. Have a way to organize these notes for easy access. You may or may not use the *aha!* in your next sermon but nevertheless write down ideas. We do this for (at least) three reasons: (a) it helps the writing process to have some ideas in print so we do not face a blank page; (b) our sermons are enriched when we have thought through our ideas and selected among them; (c) our notes are for long-term work—we may include some of these sparks or ideas one month or one year from the time we made the note.

3. ***Generate Words and Images.*** Any writing that you do will generate words and images. The brain is like a muscle and responds to activity with productivity. Here are three specific exercises that help to generate words and images. The first is to work on a *mind map*. Select a key word, image, or phrase, and write it in the center of a blank page. Then write down additional words, images, and phrases as they come to mind. Do not try to organize them or edit them, simply write them on the paper to surround the center word. They will appear as the extension of spokes from the hub of the key word or phrase. The mind map can assist sermon focus because you can begin to give weight to the ideas you want to connect and which ideas are rabbit trails. A mind map is different from an outline; you are not giving anything priority or order. Just make the connections to what is in the center and to generate thoughts. You will edit them at a later stage in the process.

A second exercise is called *writing off the page*. You need a writing implement (handheld is better than keyboard), a way to keep time, and paper. Again, select a key word, phrase, or image. Write it at the top of the page. Set your timer for five minutes (or more) and begin to write. Write down anything that comes to mind in relation to the word at the top of the page. But do not stop writing. Do not remove your pen or pencil from the page even if you must write nonsense words. If you lose concentration the continued writing will bring you back to focus.[7]

A third exercise is *daily journaling*. This is a longer-term commitment to write a certain number of pages each day. You decide the place and time, though it is helpful to keep these consistent. And you decide if you will write using a computer or with pen and paper. Generally people try to write two or three pages each day, on any subject. The point is to habituate yourself to written expression. Again, do not edit as you write. Let your thoughts go to print and later edit any of the material that you choose to use in the sermon.

4. **Connect with Your Senses.** Some biblical texts are narrative: there are characters, a setting, and a plot. We can easily imagine the sights, sounds, tastes, touch, and smells of these texts. Most of us can imagine the feel of the heat when the Samaritan woman drew water at noon in the desert. Additional research will help us connect our senses to the scenes we can't imagine. We can study the temple sacrificial system as background to Jesus' prophetic words about the destruction of the Temple. We can imagine the behind-the-scenes fighting when we study Paul's words to the Corinthian church about how they share the Lord's Supper. Words and images that invoke our senses help us connect with the text. And this imaginative work can even be pivotal in forming the focus of a sermon. We do this imaginative sense work and keep in conversation with all other textual work and theological claims. But sense language is one way of making abstract ideas become tangible.

Again, this imaginative work helps us to do two things. It helps us sift through our ideas for a sermon and hone a claim. But it also is generative and expands our thinking to make associations that are necessary for preaching to engage real life. You can select one of these exercises and determine your goal. Perhaps you want to work with a mind map in order to gain more focus. But you can also use a mind map in order to generate nuances to your key word or image. You can practice imagining the sights and sounds of texts in order to play with possible sermon ideas. But you can also do sense work in order to give a tight focus to one idea in the sermon. Practice these exercises and learn how they work. Then you will become aware of their value in the sermon preparation process.

Writing Words and Imagery

We write in order to write. We may not know what we are writing about yet. We may not have the sermonic movement or focus figured out yet, but it is necessary to start writing. And when we begin writing, it is necessary to let go of our internal editor. Anne Lamott says:

Almost all good writing begins with terrible first efforts. You need to start somewhere. Start by getting something—anything—down on paper. A friend of mine says that the first draft is the down draft—you just get it down. The second draft is the up draft—you fix it up. You try to say what you have to say more accurately. And the third draft is the dental draft, where you check every tooth, to see if it's loose or cramped or decayed, or even, God help us, healthy.[8]

Here are some ways to begin.

1. **Set a Time.** Writing in order to write is beyond difficult. Pick up any book on writers' advice about writing and you hear the siren's wail. Writing is hard. One help is to choose a time of day to write and stick to this choice. Another help is to set the duration of the writing time. Forty-five-minute blocks of time are productive. Then take a break, even a two-minute break. A break outside is best. But get a timer, set it, and write. You want uninterrupted time, focused time, timed time, pen-across-paper or fingers-to-keyboard time.

2. **Check Your Notes.** You have notes about your textual research. You have written down imaginative associations. You may have completed a mind map or a written page about a key word. You have a preacher's notebook or a file of other musings from your general observations about the world, creation, human beings, or the six-o'clock news. You will look at a blank page, but you have a compilation of notes by your side. Set the biblical text out in front of you, too. Then begin to write about those notes that seem most significant to you.

3. **Imagine the People.** It is easier to write a sermon when you can envision the listeners. As you sit down with the biblical text and your initial notes, think about the people who will hear this sermon. You may know them or you may have to do some research about their congregation to get sense of who they are. Do they know you? As you write, imagine what they know about the text at hand. Imagine what examples or stories might resonate with them. When I preached in upstate New York, the congregation had plenty of connection with analogies about snow and subzero temperatures. But I live in central Texas now, and there are different connections to be made.

3. **Detachment.** Once you begin writing do not immediately use the delete key or find the "track and change" computer command. First, a little detachment is in order. Dorothea Brand, writing about the writing process, advises, "Put it away, and if your curiosity will let you, leave it alone for two or three days. At the very least let it stay unread overnight."[9] Brand is speaking about longer-term writing projects, not weekly sermons. We cannot leave our sermon draft alone for two or three days; this is not the timeframe most preachers work with. But her point is well taken: a sermon written on Saturday night will not be fully developed. Yet we need to be able to leave our sermon draft alone overnight, or for a better part of a day. At least for a long walk. Then we can return to it with topped-off energy.

4. **Work on Imagery.** There are many forms of evocative language, of imagery. But here are four forms of imagery that you can work on when you write a draft of a sermon.

A. *Metaphor.* Metaphor is a form of thought that occurs when we use one word to mean another word. It is more than substituting a word with a synonym. Instead, in a metaphor, two things that are unlike are said to be identical, A = B. "Her life is a fishbowl" is metaphoric speech. Someone's life can't be a glass container that holds water and fish. But this type of speech creates a new unit of thought and alters the way we think about something. So now we think about this woman and know that her life is on display and everyone can see what is going on in her life, as if she is living in a clear glass bowl, able to be observed at any angle. Of course, explaining a metaphor makes it lose its punch.

Metaphors do more than make a connection between A and B; they expand our thinking. Building on a biblical metaphor in John 6, one prayer before meals says, "Blessed be God who is our Bread . . . "[10] The connection between God and bread shifts our conception of God because we are used to language about God providing bread. But it is a metaphor and is a deep way of expressing reality. This is important: metaphors are not decorative additions to speech but are a central form of human communication. Neurological research says that they are a primary way of organizing experience and expanding our conceptual, analytical, and synthetic skills.

I might say more accurately that metaphors are useful, perhaps even necessary, to unite the cognitive and emotional meaning of a proposition. The way the two are integrated has everything to do with the way our brains work. Metaphor's resonance comes from its ability to activate not only the cerebral cortex's cognitive and sensory networks, but also the limbic system's affective and motivational networks. Both systems are necessary for what we would call understanding . . .[11]

So we work on metaphorical speech. Take Scripture as your guide. God is a rock, a wall, and a storm. Jesus is bread, water, a shepherd, and a gate. The Holy Spirit is fire, wind, and a bird. Build on these metaphors. What else can you say about God, guided by the text you work with? What can you say about us, guided by imaginative speech? Try this: list ten nouns on a piece of paper. Write them down in this form: My/The ___ is a ___. The ten nouns come first and the image comes last. My life is a . . . ; My car is a . . . ; The daily news is a . . . . Begin to experiment. Then experiment with the focal ideas and images from the text you are working on. This is part of your sermon preparation, and you can still edit.

When you practice making metaphors you will begin to see them all around you.

B. *Story*. Stories are accounts of an event or events, factual or fictional. They are shorter than novels and follow a narrative plot with a beginning, middle, and an end. They have characters and a setting. It is common now for homileticians to study stories for the ways that they function as imagery: they elicit experiential connections, sensory memory, and recognition. In other words, stories carry meaning and can carry the whole experience or idea of a sermon.

Stories must be crafted with care. They do not simply speak one point. They invite multiple meanings and create new ones as we take them in. As listeners we focus on different details in the story. I will hear something different from what my husband hears even when we listen to the same story. And stories are *generative*, which means that hearing one story makes us think of other stories. A story about your parents will make my mind wander a bit to think about my own parents. There's a lot going on in the listeners' minds when preachers tell stories.

The use of self in stories is attended to in the next chapter but this can be said here: even if you tell a personal story you must still craft it with care. What is the primary focus? How many details do you include or will some secondary details trump the primary detail you want to set out?

These are the sorts of questions raised by storytelling—whether or not it is our own story that we tell.

There are other details to think about. There is *timing* (perhaps you tell the ending first and then go back to relate the beginning and middle). There is *point of view* (see *Person* later in the final chapter). There is *length*, a whole sermon can be a narrative (factual, fictional, biblical) or the story narrative can be a smaller component of the whole sermon. There might be *dialogue*, set out as ordinary speech that we really can recognize.

Stories that come at the beginning of a sermon can function as an advance organizer, a key to the way that the preacher will unfold the content or experience of the sermon for the listeners.[12] But stories poorly selected or told can be extraneous and irrelevant; we don't need a magician's puff of smoke to get our attention. If you tell a story, make it integral to the content and purposes of the sermon, wherever it comes in the sermon. It is never decoration. Story needs to be weighty enough to bear the same theological claims you make in other forms of language. A good way to check this is to look at a theological claim[13] and see if the story is a way of showing what that theological claim looks like walking around.[14]

So here's a way to begin working on stories for preaching. Select a biblical story and tell it from the point of view of one of the persons in the story. Or work with that same story and tell it from your point of view as a bystander.[15] Practice telling contemporary stories, too. When you make a note about something in your preacher's notebook, try to put it in story form later on. You need a beginning, middle, and an end. You need characters. You need a setting. And you don't come to this work empty-handed. You have your exegetical notes and your imagined associations. Try to put some of your associations in story form and see what happens.

C. *Similes and Analogies.* You can use a *simile*, which is a form of speech that makes a comparison between one thing and another thing using the words *like* or *as*: writing is like pulling teeth. The comparison helps describe or explain the object or the idea. Writing is painful, says this simile. It is hard work. Analogies are related to similes—they extend the comparison by adding more detail to it: writing a sermon is like Jacob wrestling an angel for a blessing. The story of Jacob and the all-night wrestling match is used to describe the sermon-writing process. This is a popular analogy for preaching! Similes and analogies are helpful because they are ways to make connections to our lives.

Go ahead and write down similes and analogies that come to mind. Then check them to make sure they function in the sermon the way you need them to function: Are they a main focus? Or do they need simply to serve one part of the sermon and not be so flashy that they take over the focus? Are they beneath the dignity of preaching and the biblical text or can they stand up to questions if you need to explain why you chose to use them? It is good for preachers to think through these aspects of language so that if someone asks why we chose that particular metaphor, story, simile, or analogy, we can speak to the reasons for our choice.

D. *Examples*. Examples are another form of imagery because they help us connect an idea to our lived experiences. These are neither full narratives nor stories, but instead are quick, brief phrases that help us get our bearing as listeners because, again, you have shown us what the theological point looks like walking around. These may come from your life (though see the section on *Self-Disclosure* in chapter 5) or from the world around us, or from your imagining. Specific examples are different from general examples because they include more information like place, time of day, weather, persons, and other specific details. General examples are the mention of human rights' protests or water pollution. Specific examples will tell about the protests in Tehran or giardia levels in a local water source.

Think about your listeners as you select examples. If your sermon mentions water pollution, you can give several different, brief examples that will connect to different listeners (those who worry about safe water for children; those who pay attention to global water issues; those who think anew about lawn chemicals and observing water restrictions during a drought). Look over your sermon draft and identify a concept or focal idea that you want to highlight or be certain to connect to our lives. Write down that word or idea on a separate piece of paper and then play around with a list of examples to show what it means for our lives now.

Preparing the Manuscript with Words and Imagery

You have researched many aspects of the biblical text, and you have made notes about words and images. You have even written draft portions of your sermon. But now it is time to think about the sermon manuscript.

Not every preacher agrees on the *concept* of a sermon manuscript. Some even claim that any sermon event that makes use of a manuscript is not true preaching. If that claim refers to a person hunched in a pulpit (or away from the pulpit), bending over papers so that the congregation only sees the top of the preacher's head as the preacher reads the manuscript as a maintained drone, then it is difficult to disagree. But that is not the image here.

Many preachers see the *unity between the manuscript and the preaching event* and call a manuscript an "arrested performance"[16] or "second orality." Charles Bartow speaks about this dynamic relationship of manuscript (written text) to oral/aural event when he describes the public reading of Scripture as ink being turned back into blood.

> The God of whom the Bible speaks, and whom it addresses when it speaks, is present to the speaker in the text, and present with that speaker to us who read and hear what the biblical speaker says. Just so the human experience of the God of the Bible becomes our own. With startling clarity T. S. Eliot indicated what is going on in all of this when he remarked that it is the purpose of literature to turn blood into ink. William Brower was no less vivid and on target when he said that the purpose of speaking literature is to turn the ink back into blood.[17]

Here we focus on the preparation of a sermon manuscript as a written text that is in service of the oral/aural event. This preparation happens in a variety of ways. Some preachers make an outline of the sermon's moves and preach in reference to the outline. Some preachers draw a series of pictures that remind them of the order of the sermon. Some preachers make a few notes, perhaps writing out quotes that they want to use. Some preachers do not refer to anything written except Scripture. And some make use of a full manuscript, hoping to say every word that is written down in the sermon manuscript. Some simply adopt what a mentor or supervisor does. Some experiment during preaching classes.[18] Preachers make choices about their use of manuscript. Many preachers find that the ways that they use written material to aid the preaching event changes during the course of ministry—part of the seasons of the preaching life.

The idea of the manuscript has changed over the years. One way to think about this is to compare the other forms of manuscripts that we prepare. It has been common practice that sermon manuscripts look like the pages of a term paper or a classic novel. The words fill the page. The margins are even. Sentence construction follows the letter of the law of proper grammar. But these days we are familiar with writing contexts beyond the formal letter, the classic book, and the term paper. We have blogs and e-mail, chat rooms, manga comics, and text messaging. Our words don't always fill the page. We don't always use complete sentences—or even complete words. We know about a new kind of shorthand; much of our writing more closely reflects our speech. With this in mind, we will focus on a full manuscript that won't look like a term paper. We'll start with sermon length.

Determining the *length* of a manuscript in advance is important—it helps us set a clear goal for our preaching preparation work. Typed in a twelve-point font such as Times New Roman, a single-spaced page becomes about five minutes of the oral preaching event for most preachers. This is a good general guideline for figuring out sermon length. Four single-spaced pages will be the written aid to the twenty-minute sermon. This is the painter's canvas for the preacher: we think about our preaching context and the fitting length of the sermon and we prepare the written manuscript accordingly. Some preachers use the word-count tool on their computer and calculate the length of a sermon on that basis—they have figured out the approximate number of words they speak per minute.

While looking at single-spaced pages of twelve-point font helps us determine length, sermon manuscripts we carry into the pulpit should not look like a page in a book or essay that we submit for a class. Sermon manuscripts should be *written and laid out to serve an oral event*. This is one way our twenty-first-century computer experiences help us reenvision the word in print. For example, preachers should experiment with font size to what best aids their eye when preaching. The best choice will depend not only on one's vision but also on the angle of the pulpit desk (or whatever we use to support the manuscript—hands, music stand, Bible). It may depend on the break in our bifocal eyeglasses. It will depend on the lighting in the preaching space. But the preacher can begin by exploring font size—16? 18? 24?—and what spacing works best for their vision in their contexts.

In addition to experimenting with font size and spacing, preachers should find a way of laying out the sermon text that best aids their delivery. Sermon manuscripts do not need to be printed out with the left margin justified in a straight line down the page and the right margin determined by automated returns. Instead, preachers can make use of *sense lines*.

A sense line
   is the spatial organization of a phrase or sentence
     according to the pace,
      and balance,
        and the thoughts to be conveyed.

The preacher can also mix sense lines
with traditional paragraph structure (left-justifying all sentences and stretching the words to the right margin before they are automatically returned to the left to begin again),
    when it helps bring variation
     to the style of delivery.

Sense lines do something to the way we read. Sense lines make monotonous drone difficult. Sense lines instead encourage (at least) vocal diversity of pitch, tone, and emphasis through volume. Sense lines help us vocally give life to the words on the pages. Sense lines are not written for the purpose of a vocal pause at the end of each line (creating a choppy effect) but, rather, are written to help our visual and therefore oral focus on the meaning of a phrase. A phrase may stand alone, or it will be a unit of thought within the larger flow of a sentence. The sense lines are used to underscore logical units of thought. And sense lines let our eye move more easily over the page—we can find our place easily. It is more difficult for the eye to constantly travel left to right and jump back again to the left for the next line.

There are *other manuscript prompts* that aid the delivering, instead of the reading, of the sermon. Some preachers use colored pencils or markers to demarcate the manuscript in certain ways. Some write a word or phrase in the margin next to each paragraph or section to help them—at a glance—keep track of the unfolding movements of the sermon. Some preachers put a key word in boldface and central phrases in italics in each paragraph. Many preachers have learned to print out the manuscript for only a portion of each page rather than down to the normal bottom margin. This spatial arrangement makes for easier eye contact—the preacher does not need to look all the way down to the bottom of the page. And, depending on the angle and size of the pulpit desk, some do not even use the normal 8-1/2"-by-11" paper but use half-sheets turned sidewise. The manuscript does not need to look like a term paper. It works better as an aid to the oral event if it is composed to serve orality.

Editing Your Words and Images

Preachers must make choices about words. This seems obvious, but sometimes this principle gets lost as the preaching event draws near. Preachers can get into a time crunch and grasp onto anything to show for their labor, but they should use words to create and sustain a sermon focus. This means that we do not *simply* say in the pulpit what comes to mind in our study, but we *choose* our words for specific purposes. We work toward a focus; we work to use words that will aid the sermon's unfolding. We work, by our words, toward the main event or idea of the sermon. One homiletician speaks in terms of the red thread that moves through a sermon—it is the preacher's (and, we intend, the listeners') identification of the sermon's path.[19] The red thread is the flow of the focal idea or movement in the sermon. The sermon form aids this, of course. But word choices are central. We make choices about key words and images, about transitions and signposting (more on these word activities in the final chapter). We repeat words because we want to emphasize that concept. We reiterate words because we have built them up in a way that they can hold a definition, and even comparisons and contrasts ("living water" can evoke both moving water and still water). The images hold claims about human pain and need and suffering, and the textual images hold truth about the triune God's merciful present activity in our lives and in our world.[20] But we hone our words for sermon focus. Linda Clader describes this:

> All of this means that some of our words end up on the cutting floor. We do edit. Once I've figured out what the sermon is trying to be, I start carving away extraneous material that only serves to confuse. The cartoonist Sandra Boynton has been a great help to me here. In her book *Chocolate: The Consuming Passion*, she describes the "old-fashioned" way of making a chocolate rabbit. She says, "Stand on end: 1 block of chocolate, 4 x 4 x 7 feet. Chip away all pieces that do not contribute to overall impression of rabbitittity." The parts I chop away are all still chocolate. They can be melted down and used again or just nibbled on for my personal enjoyment. But at this point the rabbit's what is important.[21]

What follows is an editorial to-do list. It is lengthy and cannot be done all at once. But make yourself familiar with it, and then these editorial insights will become a natural part of your sermon preparation process.

- *Identify your red thread.* Summarize the sermonic claim—
  what are you trying to say?

- *Summarize each paragraph with a word or phrase and edit
  for flow of thought.* This is a practical way to check the progression of your sermon claim.

- *Vary the sentence structure and length; use more short sentences.* Sermons are not essays and should not include long
  sentences. We are more able to hear short sentences and we
  certainly need variety.

- *Use small words rather than multisyllabic words.* Some
  preachers use multisyllabic words for effect and often
  repeat these words several times during the sermon. This
  works well. But use small words, too—we easily grasp their
  meanings.

- *Write like you talk or similar to how parishioners think and
  talk.* This means shorter sentences, use of contractions (I'll;
  We'll) and sentence fragments. And use active verbs (the
  subject acts instead of being acted upon), which convey
  immediacy.

- *Do not use technical jargon. . . . unless the point is to hear it
  explained so that it is introduced and learned.* We need to use
  the vocabulary words of the faith: sin, salvation, faith, justification. But preachers must show what these words mean.

- *Use correct grammar and grammar fitting for the preaching
  context.* You will have schoolteachers and many others congregants who appreciate good syntax in your sermon.

- *Use vivid words (nouns, verbs)—use less of adjectives and
  adverbs.* A walk can be a stroll or a power walk or a saun-
  ter. Pick nouns to show us specifics. A child can walk into a
  room, or gallop, skip, shuffle, or twirl. Choose verbs to show
  us details.

- *Employ pauses like we do in daily conversational speech.* Pay attention to how people use pauses in daily speech. See how pauses help mark transitions of thought and highlight important ideas. Write a note in your manuscript to pause briefly at key points.

- *Avoid parenthetical statements.* These are brief statements that modify the meaning of something you just said. If you use them you need to use tone of voice and pacing to help us hear what they modify.

- *Focus on one idea per sentence (or paragraph!).* This is a helpful rule of thumb so that listeners are not overwhelmed with ideas.

- *Make use of the conversation test.* Review your sermon writing and look at how you convey ideas. Ask yourself, "How would I say this to my friend or parent?"

- *Round off statistics.* Numbers are difficult to take in. Instead, give us a comparative image for the numbers. The overall aim is to hone your sermon focus and cut out the fat. This list provides specific editorial insights to help this work.

Planning for Long-Term Work with Words and Images

All of the work described above will become a regular part of your sermon preparation process with practice. It may look long and involved now, but it will become familiar and second nature with repeated use. Really. But there are also some practices that you can engage over time that will strengthen your use of language in preaching.

A basic principle is that we work with words to form habits. It may seem strange to talk about forming habits when it is obvious that we want to cultivate our imagination and innovation around word work. But habits are what we want. Brain science tells us that our hippocampus is full of patterns and habits and that we can create new habits. When we act in new ways and repeat those new actions, our brain actually creates parallel synaptic roads, even new brain cells. We put down new pathways.

Our old paths may have formed us to say, "Words escape me," or " I can't find the words," or "I don't know how to put this." Intentional work with words will lay down new paths within us—we can expand how we work with words in our sermons.[22]

Again, we do not commit to new habits and work with words in order to dazzle, seduce, or overwhelm listeners. We do not haphazardly stitch sequins to our sentences. Instead, we do this work because we know something about the pull of evocative language; the medium as the message; the possibilities images create. To try new things with words in the service of proclamation is to receive the gift of language as art and expression, and to believe in the power of language to evoke and transform.

We can divide this habit-forming word work between long-term and short-term work. *Long-term habits* are our ongoing work with words that helps us expand our way of saying things. You can do these things in the course of a week, but they are not done in order to produce payoff for that week's sermon. They are done repeatedly so that, over time, they repattern our capacity for working with words. Here are some suggestions for long-term habits to nurture:

- Read poetry

- Read excellent literature

- Read poetry and literature aloud to yourself

- Write letters to friends or relatives

- Ask of everything, "What does this have to do with preaching?"

- Review your preaching manuscripts for clichés and overused words/phrases

- Write every day—at least two or three pages—write anything

- Acquire a curiosity for the derivation and history of words

- Find multiple ways to speak about the same thing

- Play word games

- Listen to people talk

- Talk with small children

- Pay attention to the concrete circumstances of life

- Assign yourself a writing topic and write anything about it for a set time

- Pick a word and write two pages about it without using the word (grace, forgiveness, etc.)[23]

All of these long-term exercises are not for the purpose of finding sermon examples. We do not read poetry so that we will find more quotes or put our sermons in rhyme schematic. Nor do we engage one of these exercises to mimic it in the sermon: we do not write letters because we want all our sermons to sound like letters. We will not speak like three-year-olds for the duration of the preaching event. But each of these activities expands our vocabulary, style, and imagination and, most importantly, helps us hear and see the world differently.

There are many to-do lists in this chapter. But begin to work with these exercises. Choose a few to start with. Then incorporate the other exercises. Over time they will become a part of your sermon preparation process.

The remaining chapters include a sermon with remarks about the sermon preparation process according to the exercises named in this chapter. And the final chapter is a collection of additional word topics related to sermon work.

Our words matter. Our preaching words are vital—some of our traditions even say they are a means of God's presence in our midst. These are reasons enough to make sure you have time to work with the language of the sermon.

For Further Reading

Childers, Jana, ed., *Birthing the Sermon: Women Preachers on the Creative Process*. St. Louis: Chalice, 2001. A collection of essays and sermons by women preachers. The essays focus on these preachers' creative processes—how they go about preparing to preach. Some prepare a manuscript, others prepare to preach with no manuscript or notes. But each writer reflects on her pattern of preparation. Women from different denominations and faith traditions contribute to this book.

Clader, Linda L. *Voicing the Vision: Imagination and Prophetic Preaching*. Harrisburg: Morehouse, 2003. A homiletician writes about the work of the Holy Spirit in preaching preparation. This book includes examples from Scripture about the ways that the Spirit works with humans and suggestions for how we can stay in tune to our life in the Spirit as we work on our sermons.

Dillard, Annie. *The Writing Life*. New York: Harper & Row, 1989. Dillard's name is important among writers, and here she writes about her craft.

Goldberg, Natalie. *Writing Down the Bones: Freeing the Writer Within*. Boston: Shambhala, 1986. This writer talks about her writing process and gives examples of creative writing exercises.

LaRue, Cleophus, J., ed. *Power in the Pulpit: How America's Most Effective Black Preachers Prepare Their Sermons; More Power in the Pulpit: How America's Most Effective Black Preachers Prepare Their Sermons*. Louisville: Westminster John Knox, 2002; 2009. Two collections of essays and sermons by African American preachers from different denominations that focus on the processes these preachers use to prepare sermons.

Lamott, Anne. *Bird by Bird: Some Instructions on Writing and Life*, New York: Doubleday, 1994. Lamott's work is well known to writers and many pastors. Her writing instructions translate well to preaching.

Ramshaw, Gail. *Reviving Sacred Speech: The Meaning of Liturgical Language*. Akron, Ohio: Order of Saint Luke, 2000. Ramshaw focuses on liturgical language and its sacred and metaphorical nature. Even though this is focused on words in worship her work is a clear look at the metaphors that govern our faith practices.

Troeger, Thomas H. *Imagining a Sermon*. Nashville: Abingdon, 1990. Troeger explores the ways that imagination works and shows how processes of consciousness help preachers evoke and interpret faith in God.

Chapter 4

Preaching Words in Action
A Sermon with Language and Imagery Commentary

This sermon was preached in the San Francisco Theological Seminary (PCUSA) chapel on the Tuesday before Thanksgiving in 2007, the final service there before the holiday break. The worship service was a Word service (not Word and Sacrament). The chapel is basilica style—rectangular with raised chancel area. The baptismal font was placed in the center aisle in the midst of the nave. The gathered community included students, faculty, and seminary staff. I knew many of the faculty and staff because I had lived on campus during my doctoral work at the Graduate Theological Union in Berkeley. Many of them knew I had left San Anselmo (where SFTS is located) for a teaching position at Lancaster Theological Seminary in Pennsylvania. The reference to Lancaster comes from those years. A few other contextual notes: the *Chronicle* is the major San Francisco newspaper; the oil spill in the San Francisco Bay had happened only twelve days earlier. The news reports continued to unfold the number of species affected by the spill, the volunteer efforts, and the estimates about the damage to the ecosystems.

The text for the day, Isaiah 25:6-9, was chosen specifically for this service. Please note that the sermon has been laid out according to sense lines, as explained in chapter 3. Following the sermon I offer some commentary on the sermon that explains how I intentionally employed specific language and imagery, according to some of the guidelines I laid out in chapter 3.

The Sermon

San Francisco Theological Seminary
November 19, 2007
Isaiah 25:6-9

> On this mountain the LORD of hosts will make for all peoples
>> a feast of rich food, a feast of well-aged wines,
>> of rich food filled with marrow, of well-aged wines strained clear.
> And he will destroy on this mountain
>> the shroud that is cast over all peoples,
>> the sheet that is spread over all nations;
> he will swallow up death forever.
>> Then the Lord GOD will wipe away the tears from all faces,
>> and the disgrace of his people he will take away from all the earth,
>> for the LORD has spoken.
> It will be said on that day,
>> Lo, this is our God; we have waited for him, so that he might save us.
>> This is the LORD for whom we have waited;
>> let us be glad and rejoice in his salvation.

* * *

Our November harvest feast is three days away.

This week, our harvest practices are focused and even scripted:
    there is the turkey meal,
    maybe the intentional collection of canned goods
    or hours spent at a shelter serving the Thanksgiving meal.
    The grocery stores now display their quick access ingredients;
    the *Chronicle's* food section blesses us again with the best turkey cook-
        ing recipes and techniques.
The starter gun has fired and we are off and running for the official 2007
holiday season—our November harvest feast the first stop. Whatever
your plans, it is happening all around you.

But we also know this: fewer among us are persons who actually harvest.
   Steady a plow,
   turn soil,
   fire up a tractor,
   scan the market prices for grain,
   count and weigh what is pulled up from the earth.

A few years ago in Lancaster, Pennsylvania, we went many weeks with no rain. Then the rains came. They were multitudinous and we just about danced. But we weren't thinking about the crops.
One rainy day the newspapers told us what the continuing storms meant for our Amish neighbors—one more storm would make it impossible for them to bring in the year's corn.
But the story had good news: their bishop gave them dispensation and they were permitted mechanical means to harvest the crop that year: they beat the storm. We urban-dwellers easily forgot about the harvest even though we were surrounded by cultivated land.

Not so many of us live the cycles of harvest anymore. Instead, at least here, most everything is always available—our grocers have multiple suppliers. And, these available goods come to us wrapped and labeled—redacted, we might say.
   What is the *sitz-im-leben* of asparagus?
     Does it grow underneath or above ground?

There is a new dynamic, too—for now we are supposed to know something about our food miles and their carbon footprints:
   Just how much energy was expended to grow and transport your
     butternut squash?
   What about the oat flake cereal in the breakfast bowl?
   Is farm-raised fish really fish anymore
     or is it now the corn that it eats?

What was cyclical—and completed under the light of October's full moon—is now governed by genetic engineering, immigrant worker politics, water rights, and dispossession.

It is difficult to know about harvest these days.

What we do know something about is anti-harvest. Not plenty, but depletion.

In the Bay Area these past weeks we have been face-to-face with anti-harvest.
It is the oil.
Attached to currents and tides, it has wrapped around cliff bases, pushed to beaches.
This anti-harvest leaves an
    unproductive
        uncultivatable wake around us.
There is no more gift of plenty for
    the salt marsh harvest mouse,
      for the dunlin or whimbrel shorebirds here to feed just below the bay
        surfaces,
      for the Chinook salmon on their fall run toward Sacramento,
      for the diving ducks,
      or for the Dungeness, the oysters, their fishing boats, those livelihoods.

This sudden and visible anti-harvest has wearied the environmentalists and scientists, this anti-harvest begat accusations, legalities. The food chain damaged, anti-productive, dealt death.

We know a lot about anti-harvest. We live in its mire.

Isaiah tells us about the anti-harvest he has seen. He speaks about the Southern Kingdom—in what year? It is hard to know. Yet this is true: the Judah that Isaiah speaks to has a familiarity about it. For over the expanse of the prophetic book, this mouthpiece of the Holy One sees
    the anti-harvest of military coalitions, of wartime invasions;
    the anti-harvest of exile and military destruction;
    of empires encircling and bearing down.

The anti-harvest for Isaiah is the cycle of depletion, the cycle of burned homes and refugee camps, it is the cycle of orphans and bitterness. It is a cycle cultivated internationally, geopolitically.

Just a few prophecies preceding this one Isaiah cries out in high decibels against the whole earth drying up and languishing—anti-harvest is for him also a drought and all creeping and crawling things, all humans, die in its clench.

This is the thing about anti-harvest—it is its own cycle. It is the cycle of ongoing depletion. Anti-harvest is not only death. It is the ongoing cycle of depletion that is perpetuated around us—the oil slick, the wars, people of low food security.

A columnist used a phrase this week that I like very much: outrage-fatigue. He made the distinction between reactionary whining, on one hand, and informed, smart outrage. We have so many things to be enraged over, he said—and that the sheer volume is overpowering us—we are too weary, unable to keep up a protest.

Those of us assembled here have a list, I'm willing to bet: outrage-fatigue.
     On it for some of us is our war.
     Last week the national news made many of us list also the lack of men-
          tal health care for traumatized soldiers.
     For others it is the fatigue over pre-primary election debates.

We have our outrage-fatigue lists; our anti-harvest/oily mire lists, some-times our lists are embarrassingly personal because we have lost energy to think past ourselves. We confess that we are not productive in the way we truly want to be; not full of plenty, our storehouse depleted.

Isaiah lifts up our faces to Mt. Zion.

On this mountain, he says, the Lord of hosts will make for all peoples a feast of rich food,
     a feast of well-aged wines,
          of rich food filled with marrow,
               of well-aged wines strained clear.
It's quite an image. A table that must have had extension after extension placed in it since it was for all people. The meats. The wines. The wines strained clear, no longer bitter. The meats with their marrow.

Do you know about marrow? It may have been a long time since anyone has placed that on a plate in front of you. Marrow comes from the innermost part of bones. It is the center of the skeletal structure—marrow is from the center of what holds things up. In that center, blood is made, red cells that transport oxygen and white cells that fight off infections. Base cellular activities for life come into existence in the marrow.

It is food from the center of things. Food to strengthen weary blood. Food to make strong and fortify the soul. This is food for action. This is food that conquers chaos and depletion. It is food that destroys death. This rich food, this wine, this marrow. It is the Lord's table-food.

Just a verse later Isaiah pairs this feast with the destroyed death shroud. He is speaking about the Canaanite myth: that chief god's yearly swallowing of the god of chaos and the god of death. But now, Isaiah says: it is no longer an annual, repeating event—it is an accomplished deed, for Israel and all nations—it is once and for all. Depletion, chaos, death: swallowed. The feast is a sign of this.

* * *

Marrow-fed, shrouds swallowed
    you and I are feasted at *this* table.
You and I, the Gentiles, of the "other" nations on this mountain, we are being soul fed here. Our oil-mired depletion is lifted, our cycles of anti-plenty destroyed. Even us warring outsiders, coalition invaders, fatigued ones, we are given food to make us new and to make us ready.

Isaiah lifts our faces to this vantage point, this laden table, this harvest. For it shows the reality that God wills for all people.

Dare we live into this? It takes eyes of faith. There is so much fatigue pressing us to disbelieve. Still the oil spills; still the wars; still the hungry.

But volunteers rush to our beachfronts, strangers extend their arms and mourn one another's losses, and here you are, studying with all your might for the work of the church. And there again is God the Holy One who has swallowed anti-harvest and fuels us past fatigue and we become the wine strained clear poured out for the world and we believe again that this feast will prevail.

Our gathering here is about this—it is about being brought again to faith. It has been said this way: our little assembly here is not an escape from the world but rather an arrival at the vantage point where we can see the world more clearly. It is not to pretend that everything is all right now—it is to gather to see clearly.

Today, through the mouth of the prophet, God's table is set in front of us so that we can see more clearly—again. Look for death swallowed up. Look with eyesight strained clear—do not be fatigued—here be fed again, these words, that water, this table, this gathering, they say the same thing—the life of the triune God for all. Look also to your Thursday table—even a little bit of food on the table, it is turned now to be a sign of the Lord's table-feast for you.

The harvest is for these days. Not for future far-off storehouse, not for end time. And now, at table, you become the harvest—marrow for the Lord's work, signs of the lifted shroud. God harvests; and you are food for the sake of the world.

Language and Imagery Commentary
Exegeting for Words and Imagery

This sermon focuses on the image of harvest, proceeding from the inter-play of the biblical text (Isa. 25:6-9) and the time of year (the Tuesday before Thanksgiving). This is the "feast of fat things" text, which is already laden with words and images to study: feast, rich food, well-aged wines, marrow, mountain, Lord of hosts, shroud, sheet, all nations, death swallowed up, God wiping away tears, the "day," waiting, joy, and salvation. The words take on more power when considered in their historic context; a time of military destruction and foreign empires invading the land. This is a promise of what is to come to these people who endure political scheming, foreign invasion, and all wartime atrocities beyond their control. There is plenty of prophetic "woe" before the reader gets to the evoca-tive promises of this passage. There are so many interesting parts of the passage: the nations (what does "all" mean?), God wiping away tears, God swallowing death (the text building on the Canaanite myth), the banquet foods, and the joy. I had pages of notes on the concepts and images. In the end I chose one image that came to me during this exegetical work: harvest. I worked with it as a summary image for the whole text.

Imagining Words and Imagery

Because of the rich words and images in the text and because of the imagistic correlation to the time of year, I had plenty to listen to during the sermon preparation time. I immediately had associations with the harvest story in Lancaster, Pennsylvania, and, of course, the ongoing news about the San Francisco Bay oil spill. And the Thanksgiving holiday was layered on to all of this. Once I focused on the image of harvest, I did work with it according to the mind-map exercise described in chapter 3. I wanted to check how it could hold the dynamics of the text and current contextual realities. The image of harvest was used as a summary concept in order to contain three things: the sense of destructive powers (anti-harvest), the banquet language of the text (harvest of food and all nations in joy), and us as God's harvest for the needs of the world.

Writing Words and Imagery

As noted above, this sermon was preached in the San Francisco Theological Seminary (PCUSA) chapel on the Tuesday before Thanksgiving in 2007. I was a visiting preacher and though I have ties to that seminary community and know several staff and faculty members, I did not know the students. So I imagined things about them: they were close to a four-day break over the Thanksgiving holiday, they were coming up on the end of the semester and final exam time, and that they would welcome hearing a call to ministry again—an affirmation of the work they were doing in seminary. There were some things I did know about them: they were collecting food items for food pantries for Thanksgiving, they were aware of (and some where involved in) the clean-up efforts after the oil spill in the San Francisco Bay. In addition, the day's worship service did not include Holy Communion. In this sermon I did not tell stories but developed the sermon in relation to current events (war, oil spill, sense of too many things gone wrong in the world). To develop the sermon this way, I used examples and images, with the central image being that of anti-harvest and harvest. I played around with the seminary's urban location and its relation to harvest practices, the rites of Thanksgiving in the United States, and other interactions with food production and consumption. Likewise, I worked to imagine how the listeners would relate to the concept of anti-harvest as depletion of natural and human resources.

Preparing the Manuscript with Words and Imagery

I work with a large-font manuscript (18- or even 24-point type) and sense lines. I also print only part of each page so that I don't drop my head as far down to find the words. I mark key words and phrases with either boldface or italic so that my eye can easily find them. I number my manuscript pages. The layout here does not show all of this, but imagine these manuscript markings!

Editing Words and Imagery

The first thing to say is that a sermon can always be edited. Or, more precisely, revised, in the sense of reenvisioning the way the sermon works (or doesn't work). One aspect of editing that does not show up here is the use of pace, pause, and tone. That is a form of verbal editing that happens in the spoken sermon event. So, for example, I had a sizable pause when I moved from "It is difficult to know about harvest these days" to " What we do know something about is anti-harvest. Not plenty, but depletion." That was a change of focus, and I slowed down to underscore that I was changing sermon focus. Likewise for "Isaiah lifts our faces to Mt. Zion." And, of course, the last phrase "and you are food for the sake of the world." You also see many short sentences and sentence fragments in the manuscript. And short words. I used some technical language but anticipated listeners who, week after week, hear seminary faculty and students preach. I presumed they would know *sitz-im-leben* but followed that up with a phrase to suggest the meaning (what is its setting). When I work on my draft, I do summarize each paragraph (see how short they are) and write the summary word or phrase next to each move. This is a way for me to check the progression of ideas and movement of the sermon. I tried to be specific with nouns and verbs to give the sermon a lively and contemporary sense: mainstream news about carbon footprints was just coming available at that time; in the Bay Area we had many reports about the animals affected by the oil spill so I named some of the species; I worked to name realistically the way that community was acting as harvest-food for the world.

Chapter 5

Leftover Words

This chapter is a collection of "leftover words." It is a reference list of additional language topics for preaching. Each entry includes the term, a definition, and observations about usage. Some entries include sermon examples. This reference list is not intended to provide strict instructions about word choice and writing, but here are pros and cons, seasoned reflections, and examples to discuss.

Call and Response. The form of preacher-parishioner dialogue that punctuates the movements of a sermon. This communication method occurs in many contexts of African American preaching. Congregational responses often include:

- Help 'em, Lord!

- Well?

- That's all right!

- Amen!

- Glory Hallelujah![1]

These responses are not the sum total of congregational responses—that would be too formalized and limiting for this rhythmic speech. As James Noel says, "There is no formal structuring to call and response pattern of black worship—it is dictated by the visitation of the Holy Ghost in interaction with the preacher's gifts and the overall mood of the congregation."[2] Refrains are called out; they punctuate the sermon flow of many black sermons, as described in this traditional verse:

> Start slow,
> rise high,
> strike fire,
> Sit down in a storm.[3]

These ritualized refrains are part of the natural preaching rhythm in particular preaching contexts. In many contexts the preacher calls for verbal responses ("Can I get an Amen!?"), or congregants will call out responses, even when most of the congregants are silent listeners. Dale Andrews describes the dynamic this way:

Participation in the preaching event becomes a communal activity shaping the worship experience. This worship style reflects the larger dialogical, West African oral culture. Black congregations feel free to express themselves, which is seen as meaningful participation in the preaching event. The congregation participates throughout different parts of the service, including preaching, singing, and prayer. These forms of participation range from a freely shaped cacophony to the more dialogical call and response dynamics. . . . The preached word becomes a communal activity. Usually, though, black congregations respond to the preacher when something mentioned touches upon the life experience of the hearers. The preacher enters each preaching task with this goal.[4]

Call and response is not limited to the African American church, however. A different type of a preacher-parishioner dialogue during sermons occurs in the Orthodox Church. There are ritualized refrains that demarcate the beginning of the sermon:

(Priest) Christ is in our midst.
(People) He is and ever shall be.

Or during Nativity:

(Priest) Christ is born!
(People) Glorify him!

And if you visit any Orthodox church at Pascha (Easter), whether Greek, Antiochian, Orthodox Church in America, or the rest, there is great probability that you will hear a portion of a fourth-century sermon proclaimed—the famous Easter sermon of St. John Chrysostom. Some congregations know Chrysostom's words by heart and speak them as a response to certain sections of this sermon. And you can be confident that the Orthodox priests and people will be shouting the paschal sentences during the sermon that night and throughout the next forty days (until the Feast of Ascension):

(Priest) Christ is risen!
(People) Indeed he is risen!

Some preachers who preach in contexts other than these two still make use of the rhythm of patterned responsorial. Sometimes the preacher, in the preaching moment, will teach the congregation a response based on the text and the sermon focus. Sometimes the preacher will borrow just one phrase from the traditional refrains described above. Call and response is a particular way to work with words in the preaching event.

Cliché. A word or group of words, usually figurative, that has become predictable from overuse: last but not least; slowly but surely; time-honored. (See *idiom* under *Grammar,* below.) *Platitudes* are related to clichés: they are also overused words or phrases but they offer advice or are moralistic. We might be bored with and stop listening to clichés like "You can hear a pin drop." But it is something else if we hear the platitude, "It was God's will." James Kay suggests this is how we think about the problem with using platitudes in sermons: "When the kerygma is routinely invoked as a mantra, devoid of theological interpretation and criticism, it functions 'ideologically' as a 'system of propositional truths independent of the situation, a superstructure no longer relevant to praxis, to the situation, to the real question of life.'"[5]

There is clichéd sermon speech, too. "I want to begin by . . ."; "Let us now. . ."; "This reminds me of a story I once heard." We've heard these words so many times that when the preacher uses them they become an indicator light for careless speech. You may write these words down in a draft stage but then return to them and edit them out. Identify what you are trying to do (make an introduction or a transition) and find new words.

Grammar. The form and structure of words and their ordering in speech and writing. At a base level grammatical rules aid communication through language. Words communicate but words out of normative sequence distract—the receiver must use more guesswork to make sense of the discourse. Consider how difficult it is to order food, buy train tickets, or find a place to stay overnight when traveling in a country where you know only a little vocabulary and almost no grammar. The right words, and words in agreed-upon sequence, help communication's speed and precision. In a congregation there will always be a person schooled in correct grammar, who will be distracted by dangling participles, sentences that end with prepositions, and the mistaken use of "can" for "may," or "me" for "I."[6]

Of course, strict grammatical correctness is questioned by postmodern sensibilities: Whose grammar, whose rules, whose last word? Even within the cultures of North American English speakers, there are variances in systems of grammar. In preaching, then, one must consider whether to follow some understanding of "standard English" or use grammar shared by the listeners in that particular preaching context. Grammatical correctness without grammatical colloquialisms may be offensive to some listeners just as a disregard for long-practiced grammatical rules may offend congregants. This is part of knowing the preaching context. But grammar can also be seen as art: basic patterns, rules, and traditions are learned and then any departure is an informed choice made for effect. We chose to balance the particularities of a context (all teenagers? intergenerational?) with connections to the larger church (How is our speech always corrected or enlarged to keep us in conversation beyond our local gathering?).

One grammatical issue that is important to consider for preaching is that of _colloquialisms_—informal and conversational words or phrases like the use of "you'd think" instead of "one might believe." Use of colloquial speech can make our speech seem more accessible to some hearers. To other listeners many colloquialisms are beneath the dignity of the sermon event, of humans speaking words about and for God. For instance, a preacher might describe the disciples as "hinky" followers of Jesus because, in Mark's account, they keep discussing who among them is the greatest.[7] Something is not quite right—"hinky"—about this. It is good to ask these questions about the colloquialism: Will everyone know what the word or phrase means? How long will it be up-to-date?

> The only trouble with accepting words that entered the language overnight is that they have a tendency to leave as abruptly as they came. The "happenings" of the late 1960s no longer happen, "out of sight" is out of sight, nobody does his "thing" anymore, "relevant" has been hooted out of the room, and where only yesterday we wanted our leaders to have "charisma," or at least "clout," today we want them to be "together." Be vigilant, therefore, about instant change. The writer who cares about usage must always know the quick from the dead.[8]

Another subsidiary of grammar that preachers need to reflect upon in sermon construction is *word usage*. This is about word choice that is accurate, precise, concrete, appropriate, and idiomatic.[9] *Accurate* word choice is similar to accurate grammar: it is right according to a system of language (for example, "eldest" and "oldest" have different meanings). *Precise* word choice refers to where words fit within a range of meaning ("eating utensil" and "spoon" are different ranges of precision). *Concrete* word choices are words that have color: they are not abstract ("her words conveyed anger" versus "her words stung"). *Appropriate* words are words selected with the context in mind (word choice for legal documents versus word choice for a children's book). *Idiomatic* word choice is usage that does not literally make sense but adds word color ("the cold shoulder"). Overused idioms, though, become trite speech; our eyes skip over the phrases because they are worn out and have lost power. This is a great amount of detail about words. Start with one category and review your writing and preaching. Here's a sermon excerpt that covers these categories of word usage:

> I hope you have known a prayer warrior. I have. When she died some years ago, at the age of eighty-eight, I took the plaque that had hung in her house for more than sixty years and hung it in mine. It says, "Prayer Changes Things." I fussed and puttered for a while over the question of where to

hang it. The front hall seemed so public. The dining room? Too preachy. The den? Well, it looked quite out of place over the big screen TV.[10]

This excerpt uses word accuracy (correct grammar), precision (mention of front hall, dining room, and den rather than general mention of rooms), concreteness ("fussed and puttered" rather than "I thought for a while"), and idiom ("preachy"). This is an example of how word usage creates a vivid picture in our minds.

Humor. A story, a joke, or a comment that is included in the sermon for the purpose of eliciting laughter. Humor plays to mixed reviews: some people want to be amused during sermons, others do not; many people live in the middle space. As you try to decide when humor is appropriate in the pulpit, consider these issues. (1) A sermon is not the same genre of public speech as stand-up comedy. (2) Jokes fall flat because they are not intrinsically connected to the content of the sermon—they come across as a warm-up act or a misplaced novelty. (3) Some listeners experience humor in sermons as insensitive to life difficulties and/or beneath the dignity of the purposes of preaching. (4) Some listeners expect to be amused during the sermon through clever word choice and witty insights. A conclusion: humor is difficult to negotiate. And then add this insight from Jane Rzepka and Ken Sawyer as well:

> Humor is complicated. Note that each joke used in the monologue on *The Tonight Show* on television requires the work of people in six highly specialized professional disciplines: *The Tonight Show* employs twelve "clippers" who track newspapers for material; a "comedy engineer" who decides what shape the joke should take; a "comedy stylist" who fashions the raw joke; the "polish man" (usually a woman), the joke's editor; the "timing coach"; and, finally, the "talent," that is to say, you![11]

This seems like enough evidence to send humor into the far country. Yet there is intrinsic humor in the Bible. Abraham bargains with God like a huckster. The disciples say, "Did not our hearts burn within us?" and we can hear laughter on the edge of this joyous discovery. And Jesus uses humor as a tool. Preachers who work masterfully with humor know how to spot it in the text and make connections between the folly and joy of the text and our lives. They know that a lighter mood in the sermon can help prepare the way for a serious insight. *Humor in the pulpit is effective and appropriate when it is not used as an end in itself but instead serves the greater purpose of the sermon.* This is different from telling jokes, making fun of people, or even inserting stories with verbal pratfalls. It is about recognizing inherent humor in the text, the human condition, or in contemporary situations and knowing how to reveal a humorous insight that has congruity with the weight of the sermon focus or movement. With regard to humor we can say that all things are lawful but not all things are helpful.

Inclusive Language. This has to do with the use of words and language forms for the purpose of including all persons within a specific language community. In common usage this phrase refers to the use of gender-neutral language so that both males and females are included. An example of gender-neutral language is the choice of *humankind* instead of *mankind*. The use of *mankind* to refer to all people is an example of socially constructed language that assumes that male language includes females and shapes a reality in which males and male experiences are the norm and females and female experiences are derivative, are less than male. To illustrate this, imagine how odd it would sound to use the term *womankind* to refer to all of humanity. Now apply the sense of oddity to *mankind*—do you have the same reaction? We still live and move about in a society constructed on male bias. Inclusive language is the way we pay attention to language constructs that acknowledge and include all people.

Inclusive language has other facets. It is also about precisely acknowledging the biological sex difference between persons who are anatomically male, female, and intrasex. Whereas *gender*, as described above, is a cultural category of thought, *sex* refers to the anatomical distinction between versions of the species. Inclusive language also means that we make thoughtful decisions about grammatical constructions and translations. Gender is also a linguistic category of thought. For instance, American common speech has become more neutral—not as many persons refer to a boat as a "she" as was once the case. But other languages have nouns that are explicitly female, male, or neuter and these designations do not necessarily match gender constructs or logic (for instance, in Spanish the words for "table" and "street" are feminine nouns, while those for "year" and "number" are masculine). It is important to distinguish between the noun having a grammatical assignment of gender and the thing itself being masculine or feminine.

Inclusive language also means the ways that our language is inclusive of persons with disabilities, persons of all ages, races, family structures, ethnic origins, and marital status. For instance, instead of saying "stand as able," which draws attention to those who are unable to stand, the suggested wording is "please stand." Another example is the use of "persons first" language: the person who uses a motorized chair, the person who is blind, the person who has a learning disability, Asperger's syndrome, or a hearing impairment. In addition, think about the people represented in your sermon examples and stories. Review who is present and who is missing: Are your examples always about persons who are married or who are white and middle class or educated and employed? Finally, pay attention to how you work with biblical texts that speak of paralysis, blindness, deafness, and other physical descriptions. These are often used in negative ways so that paralysis, blindness and deafness are named as sin. As liturgical scholar Gail Ramshaw writes,

> Some blind Christians are offended that their disability is appropriated as a symbol of spiritual ignorance and depravity. Others willingly offer their condition as an image of the disability we all share. . . . We have a dual task: to be sure we are not being gratuitously offensive, while at the same time offering such a plethora of images that all worshiping Christians will find, somewhere in the Sunday's liturgy, an image important and particularly appropriate for them.[12]

We work to use accurate language that reflects all the ways we are diverse human beings.

The use of accurate speech is also a theological endeavor. Exclusive language is language that categorizes in order to perpetuate certain structures and relationships: male as dominant, Anglo as dominant. The gospel of God names this as a false scandal. The gospel of God is (rightly) scandalous in that it uproots any oppressive entrenched conditions or state of affairs and shows them for what they are. God incarnate as a Jewish male of Nazareth is good news about particularity. Now we see that our very own created uniqueness is reflected in the particularity of the One who has united earth and heaven. All of this work with inclusive language is for right naming, for honoring God's created world and all diversity therein, for right relationships, and for honoring the gifts of God.

There is excessive use of masculine metaphors for God in the Christian tradition. Yet God is both beyond sex and beyond gender. We have the normative witness of Scripture with its many names for God, including the name that is not written or said by many faithful. But beyond the titles for God (*Adonai, Elohim, Jehovah*), Scripture names God as rock, wall, deer, king, refuge, lamp, judge, and more. Father is one among many metaphors for God, though many persons use it as God's primary name. God cannot be limited to the confines of our finite language: speech for God is metaphorical, and we do not have the right name for the Holy One. But in spite of language's limitations, we are still commanded to call upon God and to find ways to speak of God for the world. To be biblical in this enterprise is to search the Bible for images, to search tradition, and even to compare and contrast language for God with that of other religions and cultures.

Here are some suggestions for using inclusive language.

- Restate the generic use of the words *man, he, his, him, himself* with the gender-neutral terms *person, human, people, individuals, human, human beings*

- Use *humankind, humanity,* or the *human race* instead of *mankind*

- *Chairman* becomes *chairperson; policeman* becomes *police officer, fireman* becomes *firefighter,* etc.

- Do not use descriptions like male nurse, lady judge. If the point is to call attention to the biological sex of the person in these roles, use person-first language

- Use person-first language: the person who is blind, the nurse who is a man

- Do not use stereotypes. These include: certain jobs are only for women, others only for men; men are strong while women are beautiful; proper titles are used for men but not women (even thought they are also doctors, lawyers, racecar drivers, and head chefs); certain races are stupid, lazy, miserly, or intelligent; the elderly are always infirm and youth are always subversive

- Consider why you would single out a person by, for example, sex or race, when it has no bearing on the topic at hand

- Use "people of color" or "persons who are racially ethnic" instead of "minority people"

- Substitute *one, we, you,* for *he* and substitute *they* for third-person *he, she* (adjusting verbs accordingly for plural usage)

- Substitute (sparingly) nouns for pronouns

Irony and Sarcasm. Remarks based on the discrepancy between what is said (literally) and what is meant. In the use of both irony and sarcasm, what is said is actually intended as the opposite of what is said. But the effect of the two is quite different.

Irony is a subtle form of humor that works off this discrepancy. This discrepancy can at first be humorous, but it is a type of humor that quickly takes us to a serious place of things not being quite they way they seem. Ironic speech is a delicate device and takes some study and thought to use well. Irony is subtle, and some people do not catch the contradiction of its core. Yet some preachers recognize the ironies inherent in Scripture and build on them. Consider the following excerpt:

> The Gospel of John contains motifs which are highly ironical. Observe for example the interesting interplay on the theme of the weak and the strong. Who gives the most direct witness to Christ? An outsider, a Samaritan woman. Who claims the body of Jesus after the crucifixion? The strong disciples? No, two weak ones—Nicodemus, who comes off quite badly earlier in the Gospel, and Joseph of Arimathea. Who is the indisputable victor in the Gospel? The man crucified.[13]

The use of sarcasm is related to irony. It is the same construct as irony but has a bitter quality to it. Specifically, sarcasm is used derisively. It is a common device in everyday speech and gets a good deal of current play in advertising, movies, and on television. Poets and creative writers consider this type of speech a degradation of the more ingenious devices of irony and satire. For these reasons irony may have a place in sermons but sarcasm rarely will.

Person. This refers to the speaker, the one being addressed, or the one spoken about. There are three categories of person in the English language, each of which has a particular pronoun form and is necessary to verb forms. First-person language is "I" and "we"; second-person language is "you," meaning either singular or plural; third-person language is "he," "she," "it," "one," and "they." For many centuries homilies used second-person language with a smattering of third-person language. Then a shift occurred and some preachers began to use first-person plural speech. Then another shift took place and sermon speech began to use the first-person singular—preachers referred to themselves in the sermon. These pronoun changes are the result of answers to different questions: What is the relationship between the preacher and the listeners? Who is the person of the preacher in the preaching event? Is it appropriate for the preacher to be continuously self-referential during the sermon? Is first-person language too cloying and second-person language too autocratic?

You can begin to see the mix of issues. Some say that "we" language is refreshingly inclusive. The preacher includes himself or herself in the mix of all the things in life to which the sermon points. Others say "we" language is false because we never know who is included in "we." Eventually, they say, this language does not sound self-effacing or humble but too broad, too general. Different opinions exist regarding first-person singular language, too. Some say that "I" language is egotistical and always makes the focus of the sermon on the preacher. Others call it grandstanding. Still others say first-person singular language is helpful because of its particularity. In a time when listeners are wary of truth-claims, this first-person singular language locates the claim with the preacher and allows listeners to choose to claim that experience or truth assertion for themselves as well. Some only use "I" language in preaching when they think listeners can hear themselves included in that "I."[14]

There are many ideas about the use of person. But here is one more idea: changes in sentence structure and syntax help listeners stay tuned. Changes between first-person singular and plural and second-person plural are examples of this sort of variety. We may not be able to listen to an entire sermon that uses second person plural in every other sentence, or that uses "I" language that often. Alternating descriptive statements (no pronouns or third person) with direct speech (you) and personal speech (I) may help us listen. But these choices (and our ability to listen) are also dependent on tone. The preacher could use "you," second person plural, for a great part of the sermon. But it would make a difference to listeners whether this "you" was said in celebration or in accusatory anger. And, another nuance, too much change can get confusing. A starting place? Read others' sermons and observe their use of pronouns. Here is an excerpt from a sermon by James Forbes with the various references to person italicized:

> So it seems clear to *me* that the issue is basically about two kinds of Christians. Finally *we* come to it. Two kinds of Christians. *Some* have all of the normal trappings of the Christian faith, but when *they* hear the call of God on *their* lives, *they* are not ready to act upon that call. And every church has both kinds. And by the way, the parable does tend to be a little judgmental. So don't start squirming as if *we*'re going to have a division of the house between the wise and the foolish today. *You* will have to correct your own paper. *You* will have to categorize *yourself*. But the text makes it clear that *anybody* who claims to be a Christian, and when God calls *you* or *me* to service, to action, *our* Christianity runs to, that *we* are closer to the foolish side of things.[15]

Preaching and Visuals. Many preachers will preach concurrent with video presentations, drama, or dance. And sometimes the sermon happens before or after these events. All of these visuals may be forms of proclamation. And that is why preachers will pay close attention to how the sermon functions in relation to the visual event. Consider how preaching interacts with music and hymnody: our connection to the music can be changed because of what was said in the sermon. Or, conversely, the hymn creates a particular focus as we prepare to hear the sermon. The same interactions occur between preaching and all the elements of worship and so we consider them carefully. If the sermon is concurrent with the visual events, what is the purpose of the sermon? Is it to help us enter more deeply into the visual forms? If so, the sermon may function like punctuation—verbal proclamation here and there but not a steady stream of words in addition to the visual forms. Other issues arise, too. If the visual form presents Scripture will it be a translation of the text? Or will it be a paraphrase? Will it be the same translation that you used for your sermon or might key words be different? Some visual forms may use a different text altogether. For instance, the preacher may use Mark's account of Jesus' baptism but the drama troupe decides to read and enact Matthew's version. And how is the actual baptism portrayed in both: submersion, immersion, sprinkling? There are interpretive issues to sort through. The goal is to have a generative tension between the forms: sermons do not explain away the visual forms. Nor do we want competition between two forms of proclamation. We hope for congruency and this means that we have thought through the focus and purpose of each form of proclamation.

Quoted Material. Words said by another person that the preacher repeats in the sermon. Preachers quote poetry, hymns, spiritual songs, liturgical texts, novels, nonfiction, television shows, movie dialogue, blog postings, magazine articles, journal articles, bumper stickers, billboards, Scripture, others' sermons, and more.[16] The definition of quoted material may be extended to include other media that is used for bulletin covers or displayed on movie screens in the nave. This entry will focus on quoted words in the sermon. We quote other peoples' words because they say something well, or we want their opinion to underscore our point, or because the quote has a level of authority with our listeners. There is an ethic to using other people's words. We want to quote them accurately. We should know the context of what we quote—sometimes one sentence can function sarcastically in its context, but when it is lifted out of context it sounds like straightforward speech. We should also know if we are quoting words that are representative of the whole—for instance, are we quoting only one side of an argument that the source gives but we quote it as if it is their last word on the subject? Preachers have a responsibility to represent truthfully and respectfully the original source of the words we quote.

But we also have a responsibility to our listeners. For their sake our quotes should not be lengthy. It is too difficult to follow much beyond eight lines of poetry, some say, or a few sentences of prose when they are offered in an oral presentation. To serve our listeners we should cull the original source material and distill the essence of it—perhaps we combine a sentence from page 12 with a phrase from page 37. It is not a literal quote, but it is still true to the essence of the material and we have favored brevity for the sake of our listeners. It is best to quote the smallest amount possible. Sometimes this means that we set up the quotation in our own words—not overly explaining things but giving enough sense of context so that we give the quote a chance at a good hearing. Sometimes we have a few sentences to quote and we can break them up—they don't need to be in sequence in our sermon but work well as periodic appearances among our words. And sometimes we paraphrase the quote in order to stay in our own cadence.

To use someone else's words or ideas appropriately, we need to make sure that proper credit is given and hearers do not assume the words or ideas are ours. Quotations are quotations and not plagiarism because we give credit to the original source. It is too clumsy, however, to give a full citation in the body of the sermon. It ruins the flow of a sermon to pause and mention an author, a book title, a publication date, and a page number. We should gracefully reference the source of the quote so that citations fit with the flow of the sermon and keep the focus on the quote. Many people will say something general to identify the original source and then put the full citation in a manuscript: "One theologian says it this way," or "A biblical scholar had this idea," or "The hymnist captured this sense of things." And many people preach in settings where quoted material is a sign of the preacher's scholarly efforts, something valued by that community. In these contexts preachers may intentionally say the full name of the particular theologian, biblical scholar, or hymnist. This follows the principle that specifics are always more interesting than generalities. Others will choose to simply say the author's name, as a way of being concrete in sermonic language, introducing the author to the congregation, or acknowledging that the congregation recognizes the source.

Similar to the fact that full citation is easier to present in writing than in speech, it is harder to indicate in speech when you are quoting someone than it is in writing. There are no quotation marks in orality. As with our own words in a sermon manuscript, to speak a quote is to turn the ink back into blood. We are sensitive to why we selected that quoted material in the first place, and speak it with that interest and import. We do best to use our voice differently with quoted material (not hands raised to gesture quotation marks) to signal the beginning and end of it: shifting your tone or pace, pausing before or after the quote. We do not need to mimic the voice of the person whom we quote (if we know their sound), but we should give the quote energy and appropriate levity or gravity.

A specific type of quotation found in many preaching traditions is drawing quotes from others' sermons. There is even a tradition of preachers preaching entire sermons prepared by other preachers. At one time this often occurred when it was believed that the local preacher was not as smart as the bishop, so the bishop's sermons were circulated for use. Sometimes it was to perpetuate doctrine throughout the church's jurisdiction. Sometimes portions of older sermons were used because particular passages or stories had great rhetorical power and were kept alive through oral tradition and community memory.

Quotations, set pieces, stock phrases, and citations are not simple filler for a sermon. They should be chosen because they are somehow integral; it takes skill and artistry to make them fit with your words.

Self-Disclosure. The use of self in sermons through personal account or story. Famously, some homileticians have said "never!" speak of yourself in the sermon, while others self-disclose liberally, and still others take a middle path, arguing that use of self is a worthy form of illustration and recommend ways to proceed with caution. There is a gold-standard comment on this topic, found in an Episcopal bishop's remarks from a century ago. Phillips Brooks says that preaching is "truth through personality":

> . . . there are some sermons in which the preacher does not appear at all; there are other sermons in which he is offensively and crudely prominent; there are still other sermons where he is hidden and yet felt, the force of his personal conviction and earnest love being poured through the arguments which he uses, and the promises which he holds out.[17]

Brooks observes the different degrees to which preachers show up in their sermons. But he also believes this: our sermons will always reveal something of ourselves even if we do not relay personal anecdote, story, or outright opinion. Preaching is shaped by the way it comes through the particularity of the preacher.

Recent homiletical studies underscore this aspect of preaching. In a major study of persons who listen to sermons, interview data was categorized according to the Aristotelian classifications of communication: pathos, ethos, and logos.[18] The ethos of the preacher is always a part of the homiletical mix and is highly important to some listeners. Some listeners will want to hear the preacher's personal stories and other forms of self-reference. Even if the sermon is not full of such stories, these listeners naturally still hear sermons via that third way described by Brooks—and the character of the preacher is what carries the sermon's meaning.

There is, then, a sense in which we cannot escape preaching as an act of self-revelation. But there are ranges of how this happens, and there are demands on us to make informed choices about the use of self in preaching. Here are some cautions.

Anecdotes and stories are examples of *evocative language*, and evocative language is multivalent. This means that it is a style of expression that holds many meanings, and people will not only hear the smallest details that you set out about your life but will likely hear things that you did not even intend. This is a good reason to think carefully about what you reveal through each story. Listeners will respond in different ways to the preacher's self-disclosure. Some will respond to the insight or theme that the preacher intended. Others will hear it as a bid to win sympathy.

Here is another caution. Too much self-reference can shift the purpose of preaching toward autobiography time. Of the many purposes of preaching, this should never be on the list. Even testimony and witness in preaching is not the same thing as autobiography; testimony and witness serve a purpose of which the self is a part but that is also beyond the self.[19] Self-reference week after week brings to mind words like *self-preoccupied* and *self-indulgent*. What are your motivations for self-disclosure?

Besides revealing things about yourself, personal stories often reference and reveal things about others. Including weekly stories about one's parents, spouse, children, or pets shifts the sermon to autobiography. And to hear about former parishioners, neighbors, or local shopkeepers will raise for current congregants the question of confidentiality: If the preacher tells these stories about others, what will be said about us? The preacher must avoid stories that compromise trustworthiness.

Despite these concerns, personal stories hold potential power for proclamation. Here is Barbara Brown Taylor's argument for using them:

> The reason personal stories are dangerous and the reason I use them are the same: the voyeurism involved. People may become more interested in what I am up to than in what the text is up to, and that is where it goes awry. But what they are listening for, I think, is some evidence that they are not as crazy as they think. That is why they watch and listen to other people—to decide how normal or abnormal they really are. At least, that is what makes me a voyeur. So by using personal stories in sermons, what I mean to be doing is offering my listeners a little chunk of our common humanity, so that they can say, "Oh, you too? What a relief!"[20]

Hearers want to know that the preacher is caught up in the life of God. They do not want lectures, dry presentations, unexamined propositions. They want to put their trust in this person. They want to hear that the fire of God has passed through her or his bones. They want to hear about the ways the preacher sees God active in our midst so that they can see God as active in their own. They want to hear how the biblical texts lay claim on the preacher's life, so that they feel claimed as well.

Sentimentality. A sentiment is a feeling or opinion based on emotion, but sentimentality is a charge that something in the realm of emotions is overdone. Sentimentality is about an emotional response that is disproportionate to the events. It is writing or speaking about something in a way that aims to elicit more of an emotional response than the situation really demands. It was an older rhetorical device used in relation to a variety of emotional responses but current use relates it to tenderness, sadness, and grief. As Linda Clader warns,

> We have all rolled our eyes as a preacher milked an experience for emotional impact, playing to our heart without satisfying our minds. We do not enjoy hearing confessions that only make us embarrassed for the one confessing, and we do not like being manipulated when the manipulation itself seems to be the goal. We are looking for authenticity and honesty and courage in our leaders, and when we fail to find them, we become rebellious.[21]

Most often sentiment derails into sentimentality when we do not have congruency between the content and intention. Identify the emotional content of your sermon's evocative material and be clear with yourself what your hopes are in including that material. Preaching relates to our emotions but helps us harness the emotions for good actions.

Signposting. The use of conjunctions or connecting phrases to assist the listener with following the sermon's movement. Conjunctions normally connect words, phrases, or clauses. They include the words *but, and, because, either, neither, yet,* and others. The adverbs *however* and *therefore* function the same way. You were likely taught not to use conjunctions and adverbs at the beginning of a sentence. But we are writing for the ear and these words alert us to a change of thought or a new progression in the sermon. Preachers use these linguistically to post a metamessage that says, "Stay with me; I am making a turn." We do not need to use these transition words at every paragraph, which would be forced and predictable. But words indicating a new idea or a change of vantage point help us keep up. Preachers can introduce a shift in the sermon movement or a turn of an idea through sentence structure as well.

But there are dissenting opinions among preachers about such transitions. Linda Clader argues,

> I believe that transitions are overrated in preaching. We need to craft a transition carefully only when we are attempting to carry our listeners through a tightly organized argument—the classic-essay form. But that is not how people are accustomed to listening, it is not how we have been conditioned by the movies, and it is not the way we need to preach. The suspense built by a powerful linear narrative can also be provided by an abrupt shift to a new viewpoint or a change in setting. You suddenly bring in an apparently unrelated statement or story, and the listener—even one who has been only halfway tuned in to you—has to ask, "Now where's this going?"[22]

Look over your sermon manuscript. Identify the movement of ideas. And then see if you are using words or sentence structure to create signposting, or if you have changed tack enough that we will notice a shift in the breeze.

Sound. A literary and verbal skill of putting particular words together for the way that they effect meaning through tonality, cadence, rhythm, timbre. We could talk about air and vibrations and eardrums, but along with the physicality of making and receiving sound is word choice to effect sonority.[23] The English alphabet contains consonants and vowels. Vowels (a, e, i, o, u) can stand alone as sound; consonants need a vowel to be voiced. Consonants are divided into categories of semivowels and mutes. Semivowels at ends of syllables can continue their sound (m, r, y, as in *him, for, why*); some of the semivowels are liquids (l, m, n, and r)—they sound fluid. Some are aspirates and can only linger at the end of a syllable with the accompaniment of a sustained breath (f, c, x, g, h, j, s). Some semivowels are noisier than these (v, w, y, z). Mutes need a vowel to be sounded, and when they occur at the end of a syllable, they stop our breath (b, d, k, p, q, t).

We build from these vowels and consonants. *Consonance* occurs when a consonant at the end of a word is repeated (young, ring), and when the consonants surrounding vowels are repeated (tame, time). *Assonance* occurs when vowel sounds are repeated close to each other ("I'll grab a cab"; "She'll phone home"). An *anaphora* is the repetition of a word or phrase at the start of successive sentences (the Beatitudes are a good biblical example: "Blessed are . . ."). *Epistrophe* is the repetition of a word or phrase at the end of several sentences or phrases, one after the other. *Alliteration* is the sound of repeated identical consonants at the beginning of a word or a particular syllable. *Rhythm* is the sound between the sounds—the space between the space that sound takes. Consonants underscore rhythm. *Syncopation* is variation of the repetitive beat, the offbeat. *Stammering* can be intentional, the repetition of a word at the start of a phrase as if the preacher is unable to say the next words. There is *rate* of our speech, the *pitch* of our voice, *tone* for meaning. We may remember *onomatopoeia* from a junior-high English class—the sounds linked to a sense of the thing ("Bzzz goes the bee"). Preachers learn from poets and novelists.

Attention to language at the level of rhythm, repetition, vowels, consonants, has effect. The aesthetics of how a preacher sounds influences the meaning hearers take/make from the sermon. The microscopic work of shaping the sounds of the sermon gives our words texture, staying power, neurological impact. It evokes and makes us know things in ways beyond cognitive-rational categories.

Soundalikes. Words in the English language that are spelled differently and have different meanings but are pronounced the same. Soundalikes are not always a problem in preaching, but they can create misunderstanding if their context does not make their meaning clear. Sometimes preachers need to choose a different word to avoid confusion. An ancient liturgical hymn appointed for the story of Jesus' healing of the blind beggar (John 9) includes this phrase: "Jesus reached out his molding hand." Most of our brains flit to thoughts of mold and mildew before we think about Jesus, like a potter, shaping and forming sight. The preacher could use this phrase but would do better to change word order or add a word to help the intended meaning come through: "Jesus reached out his hand, molding the clay to press on the beggar's eyes." Another example comes from our phrasing, not a quote. We might end a sentence saying: "We are

God's." Obviously, the apostrophe doesn't translate well for hearing when it comes at the end of the sentence—so it sounds like we are claiming that "We are gods." The preacher must look over created and quoted material and make word changes to help the meaning be clear for orality. In this instance the preacher extends the grammatical contraction to "We are God's own" or changes the verb to one that expresses possession, "We belong to God."

Preachers listen to the sounds of words. Some words sound too much like other words and can be confusing. Some grammatical constructions do not communicate well. Preachers need to pay attention to soundalikes.

Stereotypes. Limited, formulaic, and oversimplified references or descriptions of a person or groups of people. The etymology of the word gives us a picture that is helpful for understanding linguistic stereotypes: a stereotype is a metal mold that printers use to produce multiple copies by casting.

Stereotypes are damaging because they reduce people to objects. A specific kind of stereotype found in literature is the use of *stock, one-dimensional, or flat characters*: the greedy lawyer, the wicked stepmother, the silent cowboy. While these stock images may live in novels and movies, they do not reflect reality. Not all—or even most!—lawyers, stepmothers, and cowboys are greedy, wicked, or silent. Our uses of stock images in conversation or in sermons do not reflect reality either. Though it is common to hear racial, ethnic, gender, and age-related stereotypes, we must work to exorcise these from our speech. This includes comments like young people are irresponsible, old people are senile, blacks have rhythm, blondes are dumb, Muslims are terrorists, and the like. Instead, think about these things: generalizations are less interesting than specifics, people are complex, and that stereotyping is a denial of humanity. Our sermonic speech can show the full diversity of the world. Begin by following the "persons first" rule: persons who are elderly; persons who are young; persons who are white, and so forth. Then edit for any ways that you assign one characteristic to a group of persons.

One extreme of stereotypes are the single words that have crept into common usage in so many nations. These are words that, by their use, degrade a person for their culture, race, gender, orientation, nationality. They are not even phrases, just a word. Some say these are the words that can never be used publicly, in worship gatherings, or even privately. There are some who challenge this stance and will use these words. In some contexts this is a generational conflict. Why would a preacher use a word known to be prejudiced, incendiary, and sure to cause someone harm? Some argue to reclaim such words. Some argue for usage so that they are devolatilized. Some say they should be articulated along with their history so we know the weight of their sin. Some live in faith-community contexts where these words are used: an intentional usage to take away the prejudice. Can such words be defused? How would you know? And is it your choice?

Technical Language. The language or idiom of a particular discipline. The technical language of preachers is theological nomenclature. We are taught concepts and given words that categorize concepts so that we can speak a shorthand of sorts. We learn words like "hermeneutics" and "epistemology" and "eschatology." We do not need to avoid these words in our preaching, but we must make sure that (1) we make plain what they mean and (2) that we are not using then for show. In all of this we balance our use of big words and technical language. We choose words for the ear, and big words need to be balanced by other types of words.

Tone. A way of writing or speaking that indicates the attitude of the speaker, consisting of use of verb tense, phrasing, and sentence structure. When we learn verbs for the English language, we learn six tenses: present, past, future, present perfect, past perfect, and future perfect. These are *normal* tones. For instance: I preach, I preached, I shall preach, I have preached, I had preached, and I shall have preached. But we have a way to intensify our verbs—we can make verb tone *emphatic* (using a form of the verb "to do" to underscore the action: "I did preach!") or *progressive* (action that is continuing at the time referred to in the sentence: "I will be preaching"). All of this explanation is to help you recognize what you are most likely already doing in everyday speech and perhaps in preaching, too. Normal-toned verbs are standard and descriptive. The emphatic tone intensifies the action and progressive tone marks it as ongoing.

Varied use of sentence structure and phrasing are other ways to determine tone in writing. Short sentences or use of phrases conveys informality and a sense of conversation. Long sentences are more formal. These are ways of working with verbs and sentence structure that give greater variety to our public speech in preaching.

Voice. In grammar voice refers to the relationship between the action that the verb describes and the subject and object of the sentence. "I baked the bread" is active voice. "The bread was baked by me" is passive voice.

Active-voice verbs emphasize the doer of an action while *passive-voice* verbs emphasize the receiver of the action. The active-voice construction is direct and brief. The passive-voice construction is wordy. It is also confusing because the emphasis is not on the one acting but on the receiver of the action. It is easy to drop the phrase that identifies the actor: "The bread was baked." Writers prefer the active voice to the passive voice. "Though legitimate for some purposes, passive constructions often give the impression of indecision, fuzzy thinking or imagining, or downright deceitfulness, as in bureaucratic and academic prose."[24] Listen for the passive voice in your sermons and work to use active-voice verbs. Somehow, many of us equate intelligence with the passive voice. It can have a dignified distance. But, more often, it is unclear, distracting, and cumbersome.

For Further Reading

Bozarth, Alla Renee. *The Word's Body: An Incarnational Aesthetic of Interpretation.* Lanham, Md.: University Press of America, 1997. Bozarth writes about speech as an incarnational act bringing text to life.

Jason, Philip K., and Allan B. Lefcowitz. *Creative Writers' Handbook.* 5th ed. New Jersey: Prentice Hall, 2009. This handbook stands out from other books of this genre. The authors are thorough and engaging writers. This book is comprehensive in the discipline.

McClure, John S. *Preaching Words: 144 Key Terms in Homiletics.* Louisville: Westminster John Knox, 2007. McClure provides a compendium of concepts that are central to the work of homileticians and preachers.

Moyers, Bill. *Fooling with Words: A Celebration of Poets and Their Craft.* New York: Morrow, 1999). Moyers interviews eleven poets about their craft.

Zinsser, William. *On Writing Well: An Informal Guide to Writing Nonfiction.* 2d ed. New York: Harper & Row, 1980). A nonfiction and humor writer instructs the reader in the art of good English.

Appendix

Theories of Communication

On the following page you see a chart titled Theories of Communication, the purpose of which is to facilitate a quick orientation to the six theory types laid out in chapter 2, namely that Preaching (a) *Communicates*, (b) *Persuades*, (c) *Tells the Truth*, (d) *Gives Language*, (e) *Interrupts*, and (f) *Transforms* (all listed in the left column). At a glance, then, you can see three comments on each theory: (1) *Basic Concern*, (2) *Basic Method*, and (3) *Purpose of Language and Imagery in Preaching* according to this theory. The *Basic Concern* column is a snapshot summary of that language theory—its core questions and concerns about the purpose and function of human language. You will notice that the first theory type, *Communication*, is actually listed as two separate theories. This is because there is such a difference between communication theories that build on *objective* understandings of language from those communication theories that build on *interpretive* understanding of language (see chap. 2). The column titled *Basic Method* is a snapshot of the central method or technique for each communication theory—that is, the way language acts. The last column, *Purpose of Language and Imagery in Preaching*, takes the core questions and concerns of each theory type and then focuses it more tightly for what it says about language and imagery in the preaching event.

This chart is intended to be a straightforward orientation to these theories. But it certainly cannot show all the nuances and complexities of each theory. Used as a summary of the material of chapter 2, it can help you remember key concerns of each theory. Used as a first-glance orientation, the chart should help you ask more questions about each theory and how they are different from each other.

Theories of Communication

Theory Type	Basic Concern	Basic Method	Purpose of Language and Imagery in Preaching
Communication (Objective)	Delivery of message	Identify and communicate content	Delivery of message
Communication (Interpretive)	Co-creation of message	Engage listeners associations	Initiate shared reflection
Persuasion	Speech that convicts	Ethos/Logos/Pathos	Teach, delight, persuade
Tells the Truth	Communicate what is knowable and true	Logical proofs Verifiable experience	Prove claims of truth
Gives Language	Identifies structural meanings	Attention to patterns in biblical texts and in our lives	Form listeners in biblical patterns
Interrupts	Questions structured meanings	Scrutinize embedded presuppositions	Open meanings
Transforms	Meaning emerges in moment of speech	Shapes speech for experience	Create an experience congruent with content

Notes

Chapter 1 • Choosing Preaching Words

1. Robert W. Hovda, *Strong, Loving and Wise: Presiding in Worship* (Collegeville, Minn.: Liturgical, 1976), 76.

2. Jean Chrysostome, *Huit catéchèses baptismales inédites*, ed. A. Wenger, Sources chrétiennes 50 (Paris: Cerf, 1957), 257.

3. Augustine, "Lying," in *Treatises on Various Subjects*, Fathers of the Church, ed. R. Je. Deferari, vol. 16 (New York: Catholic University of America Press, 1952), 109.

4. Gordon Lathrop, *Holy Ground: A Liturgical Cosmology* (Minneapolis: Fortress Press, 2003).

5. Marvin McMickle, *Shaping the Claim: Moving from Text to Sermon*, Elements of Preaching (Minneapolis: Fortress Press, 2008).

6. Personal communication, David Willis, March 27, 2008. I am indebted to his way of working with words—I can count on them to be slant. See his most recent books, *Notes on the Holiness of God* (Grand Rapids: Eerdmans, 2002), and *Clues to the Nicene Creed: A Brief Outline of the Faith* (Grand Rapids: Eerdmans, 2005).

7. Personal communication, David Willis, March 27, 2008.

8. Alice W. Flaherty, *The Midnight Disease: The Drive to Write, Writer's Block, and the Creative Brain* (New York: Houghton Mifflin, 2004), 226.

Chapter 2 • What Preaching Words Do

1. Aristotle, *The Rhetoric*, trans. L. Cooper (Ithaca: Cornell University Press, 1932), I.

2. "The grand is not the most flowery; that is the middle, which is intended for the pleasure of the audience. The grand style aims at moving the audience to believe or do what the speaker is calling upon them to believe or do." In Lucy Lind Hogan and Robert Reid, *Connecting with the Congregation: Rhetoric and the Art of Preaching* (Nashville: Abingdon, 1999), 149.

3. For instance, see George Campbell, *Philosophy of Rhetoric*, 1776; John Broadus, *A Treatise on the Preparation and Delivery of Sermons*, 1870; Kenneth Burke, *A Rhetoric of Motives*, 1950.

Chapter 3 • Weekly Word Work

1. James Forbes, *The Holy Spirit and Preaching* (Nashville: Abingdon, 1989), 75.

2. Dietrich Bonhoeffer, *Worldly Preaching: Lectures on Homiletics*, trans. Clyde E. Fant (New York: Crossroad, 1991), 121. One highly esteemed book about the creative process for preaching echoes this understanding. See Jana Childers, ed., *Birthing the Sermon: Women Preachers on the Creative Process* (St. Louis: Chalice, 2001).

3. See Mary F. Foskett, *Interpreting the Bible: Approaching the Text in Preparation for Preaching*, Elements of Preaching (Minneapolis: Fortress Press, 2009).

4. Linda L. Clader, *Voicing the Vision: Imagination and Prophetic Preaching* (Harrisburg: Morehouse, 2003), 85.

5. See Jana Childers, "Seeing Jesus," in Childers, ed., *Purposes of Preaching* (St. Louis: Chalice, 2004), 46.

6. Natalie Goldberg, *Writing Down the Bones: Freeing the Writer Within* (Boston: Shambhala, 1986), 53.

7. This is described in Jana Childers, *Performing the Word* (Nashville: Abingdon, 1998), 110.

8. Anne Lamott, *Bird by Bird: Some Instructions on Writing and Life* (New York: Doubleday, 1994), 25–26.

9. Dorothea Brande, *Becoming a Writer* (New York: Tarcher/Putnam, 1934), 143.

10. Gail Ramshaw, "Harvest," in *Treasures Old and New: Images in the Lectionary* (Minneapolis: Fortress Press, 2002), 207.

11. Alice W. Flaherty, *The Midnight Disease: The Drive to Write, Writer's Block, and the Creative Brain* (New York: Houghton Mifflin, 2004), 230.

12. Dr. David White, class lecture, Austin Presbyterian Theological Seminary, October, 2008.

13. See Marvin A. McMickle, *Shaping the Claim: Moving from Text to Sermon*, Elements of Preaching (Minneapolis: Fortress Press, 2008).

14. See Thomas G. Long, *The Witness of Preaching*, 2d ed. (Louisville: Westminster John Knox, 2005), 209.

15. Linda Clader used these examples for a workshop on preaching at Lancaster Theological Seminary in 2004. I am indebted to her insights here.

16. Childers, *Performing the Word*, 49.

17. Charles Bartow, *God's Human Speech: A Practical Theology of Proclamation* (Grand Rapids: Eerdmans, 1997), 102.

18. Barbara Brown Taylor, "God's Palpable Paradox," in *Ten Great Preachers*, ed. Bill Turpie (Grand Rapids: Baker, 2000), 129. Taylor discusses this in her interview about the sermon.

19. I first heard this phrase from Jana Childers, lectures, San Francisco Theological Seminary, Spring, 1998.

20. Gordon Lathrop, *The Pastor: A Spirituality* (Minneapolis: Fortress Press, 2006), 51.

21. Clader, in *Birthing the Sermon*, 60–61.

22. Janet Rae-Dupree, "Can You Become a Creature of New Habits?" *The New York Times*, May 4, 2008, http://www.nytimes.com/2008/05/04/business/04unbox.html, accessed September 2, 2009.

23. See Childers, "A Shameless Path," and Clader, "Homily for the Feast of the Visitation," in *Birthing the Sermon*, 35–66; see also J. Alfred Smith, "How Can They Hear Without A Preacher?" in Cleophus J. LaRue, ed., *Power in the Pulpit: How America's Most Effective Black Preachers Prepare Their Sermons* (Louisville: Westminster John Knox, 2002), 137.

Chapter 5 • Leftover Words

1. Evans E. Crawford with Thomas Troeger, *The Hum: Call and Response in African American Preaching* (Nashville: Abingdon, 1995), 15.

2. James A. Noel, "Call and Response: The Meaning of the Moan and the Significance of the Shout in Black Worship," *Reformed Liturgy and Music* 28, no. 2 (1994): 72–76.

3. Cleophus J. LaRue, *The Heart of Black Preaching* (Louisville: Westminster John Knox, 2000), 11.

4. Dale P. Andrews, *Practical Theology for Black Churches* (Louisville: Westminster John Knox, 2002) 22.

5. James F. Kay, *Preaching and Theology*, Preaching and Its Partners (St. Louis: Chalice, 2007), 28.

6. Two popular books that draw attention to grammatical mistakes in the likes of billboard slogans and subway placards in order to incite commitment to proper grammar are Lynne Truss, *Eats, Shoots & Leaves: The Zero Tolerance Approach To Punctuation* (New York: Gotham, 2004); and Patricia T. O'Conner, *Woe Is I: The Grammarphobe's to Better English in Plain English* (New York: Riverhead, 1996).

7. The Urban Dictionary, http://www.urbandictionary.com/define.php?term=hinky, accessed September 10, 2009.

8. William Zinsser, *On Writing Well: An Informal Guide to Writing Nonfiction*, 2d ed. (New York: Harper & Row, 1980), 45.

9. Philip K. Jason and Allan B. Lefcowitz, *Creative Writers' Handbook*, 5th ed. (New Jersey: Prentice Hall, 2009), 53–63.

10. Jana Childers, "A Shameless Path," in Jana Childers, ed., *Birthing the Sermon: Women Preachers on the Creative Process* (St. Louis: Chalice, 2001), 47.

11. Jane Rzepka and Ken Sawyer, *Thematic Preaching: An Introduction* (St. Louis: Chalice, 2001), 71.

12. Gail Ramshaw, *Treasures Old and New: Images in the Lectionary* (Minneapolis: Fortress Press, 2002), 267.

13. Morris J. Niedenthal, "The Irony and Grammar of the Gospel," in *Preaching the Story*, ed. Edmund A. Steimle, Morris J. Niedenthal, and Charles L. Rice (Philadelphia: Fortress Press, 1980), 143.

14. Barbara Brown Taylor, "Bothering God," in Childers, ed., *Birthing the Sermon*, 157–58.

15. James Forbes, "Are You Running On Empty? (Matthew 25:1-13)," in *Ten Great Preachers*, ed. Bill Turpie (Grand Rapids: Baker, 2000), 63–64.

16. Hymns and other words set to music are difficult material to quote; the music is part of their meaning and they are not the same without it. Nor is it the same for the preacher to sing a stanza solo (as a way of quoting) when the congregation is used to corporate singing.

17. Phillips Brooks, *Lectures on Preaching Delivered Before the Divinity School of Yale College* (New York: Dutton, 1882), 116.

18. "Everyone in the congregation hears the same sermon. But each person understands the sermon through that person's particular setting. The three settings and their main themes are drawn from Aristotle. They are:
- ethos—which has to do with the congregation's perception of the character of the preacher and of their relationship with the preacher;
- logos—which has to do with the congregation's perception of the ideas of the sermon and with how the preacher develops those ideas;
- pathos—which focuses on the congregation's perception of the feelings stirred by the sermon."

Ronald J. Allen, *Hearing the Sermon: Relationship/Context/Feeling* (St. Louis: Chalice, 2004), 2.

19. "Preaching in the tradition of testimony offers another view of the role of experience in proclamation. The preacher is called to engage the liberating power of God's word in the biblical text and in life, and then to narrate and confess what she has seen and believed in that experience." Anna Carter Florence, *Preaching as Testimony* (Louisville: Westminster John Knox, 2007), xxvii.

20. Taylor, "Bothering God," 157.

21. Linda Clader, *Voicing the Vision: Imagination and Prophetic Preaching* (Harrisburg: Morehouse, 2005), 96.

22. Ibid., 104–05.

23. See Teresa Fry Brown, *Delivering the Sermon: Voice, Body, and Animation in Proclamation*, Elements of Preaching (Minneapolis: Fortress Press, 2008).

24. Jason and Lefcowitz, *Creative Writer's Handbook*, 402.